v v v

Songs to the Sun

v v v

Table of Contents

[Stephen Hollins]

gems the colour of black

Golden Bay's Luminate festival pumps out
a kaleidoscope of cutting-edge music
& performing arts for greenie eco-warriors

a solo blindfolded farmer in heavy boots
drags a giant yellow cornfield behind him
the barbed wire digs into wrists elbows and ankles
pulling flesh as he stomps toward a river

the merchant banker in a pinstripe suit
scatters money set on fire into his smoking field
didgeridoo and gypsy violin tango-dance
to the heartbeats of bass and drum, pushing him on

from the stage, two women sing a Scottish ballad
voices of liquid gold fill the space
between thousands of ears

black is the color of my true love's hair
her lips are velvet roses fair
she's the sweetest smile
and the gentlest hands
I love the ground, whereon she stands

the sleepy sun slips behind thick dark curtains
painting skies black with punch hole diamond stars
harvest moon shines down on the old man's shoulders

face and hat froze to a coal blue stone
as his animated shadow dances behind him
whirling and leaping, a spinning top across the field

a black ghost kicking up fireballs
brass tones from spitting saxophone feed him
the same amber honey he has worked
for a whole life to harvest in the sun

harvestman's face and hands a roadmap of wrinkles
cut deep into his leathery skin, paint a country life
of hard work, sun scars, debts, death, and isolation
his luminous eyes shining gems the color of black

I am loving writing poetry! I live on Waiheke Island, New
Zealand. I specialize in Improv for Theatre, Acting,
Storytelling, Dance, Clown, Mime, Teaching, Building.
Allpoetry.com/Stephen_Hollins

[Arlice W. Davenport]

Cannon Beach

I walk along Cannon Beach at low tide.
The sea lazily laps my legs.
The tawny sand is firmly packed, pockmarked
by seagull prints. Birds are on the hunt for food.
Tiny crabs scurry past; orange-pink
starfish cling to black boulders,
plump, distorted sea creatures
are inured to the tidal pull.
A lavender-red sky signals twilight.
I head toward Haystack,
that natural icon of coal-black stone.
Ahead the path is strewn
with footprints.
I scan the horizon, alone,
then lazily make my way back home.

Cannon Beach is one of the jewels of the Oregon coast.
Though extremely popular, it retains its pristine nature.
Walking along the beach you feel the urge to celebrate beauty.
It is worth every word. Allpoetry.com/arliced

[Ursula McCabe]

Sanctuary

There are no footholds down to the river.
Scrambling past jutting old stumps
slippery with heart shaped alder leaves,
I master the primitive path.
Stumbling slightly,
landing on knees
no damage, walk begins.

The canyon sides are steep
with muddy exteriors and clay veins.
Limbless trees slide crown first downhill
and line the banks-
their upturned roots a testament
to high winds, high water
or both.

Smoothed from constant tumble,
silt covered cantaloupe sized rocks
cover the beach.
River stones gather in ovoid rings-
watery graves for exhausted Chinook salmon

Chestnut orange maples and conifer hunter green
form a harvest colored mural.
I turn my head to a kingfisher's throaty cackle
and spot something under a copse of young vine maples.

4

It's the lower jaw of a deer-
the teeth perfect chewing tools-
pointed sharp on the inside of jawline
better for stripping twigs on the go.

But the jawbone is old and has no story to tell.
I hope it was a quick death-
maybe a cougar lurking in late dusk,
too swift for this white tailed deer,
who should have been bedded down for the night.

I think of the deer, her tremulous heartbeat
pounding hard, filled with fear--
till thick blood rivulets flowed to shore.

This river and sanctuary land around it,
a place for dying--
and the living too.

Ursula in Oregon where she spends time with ospreys, blue
herons, and the occasional kingfisher. She has come to poetry
later in life, and is feeling more complete.
Allpoetry.com/Ursulawmccabe

[Eric D Grady]

Mother's Masquerade

the white and hollow loft door creeks

when I approach across waves of hardwood,
swinging open, faux brass fixtures on paned

panels squeal on ungreased hinges,

The entryway sounds so old now.

I ascend the flight of ivory berber stairs

towards the room she killed herself three days ago,
my nostrils dry with dusty heat and nicotine

caking the walls from Marlboro Lights she smoked,
each step twisting in impossible gravity

as if the architects Escher and Penrose,

I do not remember all these halls.

she looms in megalithic stature,
godlike against the horizon,

ostrich legs bent wildly,
one vertical in grotesque arabesque,

I am frozen in macabre wonder.

her skin a brilliant violet-blue lividity

matching stripes knit across a cream sweater,

denim wraps her spindled legs below the waist,
black whiskers curl in kempt

1980's fashion upon the scalp,

a purple foot dangling from her leathery wrist,
toes pointing down at the floor where she

was found forcing me to take heed,
choked by my plasticine lips and tongue

i murmur in echoes:

"I found you there
I
found
you
there"

———————————

Eric began writing poetry on Dec 13, 2018 to process
emotions spilled post-discovery of his Mother's suicide. He
will continue improving his poetry through study, writing, and
self-discovery.
Allpoetry.com/Usurp

[Marilyn Griffin]

Outline

autumnal sky
its wispy kimono of redpinks
dressed the golden fields
just left of the I-15
in this southern california fall

daughter Sallie in her scarecrow costume
straw peeking from her plaid shirt
a sharpie outline of a crow on her cheek
gathered her paints in a willow basket
for her high school choir
sponsored corn maze

at Blakley's farm the fields were ripe
with children
in almost, but-not-quite adult bodies
teasing each other around the tractor
hitched to a wagon laden with hay bales

a scripted welcome for the guests -
a mystery hayride where
you had to identify the murderer,
a vampire who terrorized victims
in the maze
stalks outlined above the stacks
while low flying banners and crows
added seasonal color

popcorn and petting zoo tickets littered
the weedy ground
as adults politely picked up trash-

the kids would sing
Madrigal songs in five part harmony
discordant with the season-
all with ladybugs or butterflies lighting
on chapped cheeks
drawn on by my girl who left her
paints in the maze
and couldn't find them-

quickly
the sun slipped behind
the shoulders of the
adolescent hills

we left-
nearly the last ones out-
searching for paints
we never found

Thank you AP for giving me space to write. I am very grateful
to all the poets who have encouraged me!
Allpoetry.com/Greeningofautumn

[Mercedes Webb-Pullman]

while stealing lemons from my

neighbour's tree

full moon flooded backyards with light
drained colour from
grey shapes

in deep shadows
something moved

an oval shape shimmered
a ripple in air
his garden still visible
as if through a window into
a different world
where colours looped through lines
making waves merge and blend on the verge of shape
then drop
disperse

bright points intersected
fused in coloured surges
built and fell in unearthly union
the multiverse working
flexing with my pulse
my breath

drawn closer

I tripped a harsh security light
the shape shrunk
as if in pain fizzing
like salt on a snail

I turned back
lost
when the vision
vanished

Mercedes lives in Haumoana New Zealand and writes about
the world and her place within it. She holds MA in English
from Victoria University Wellington
Allpoetry.com/Just_Mercedes

[David I Mayerhoff]

A Night on the Deck

Sitting crusted in
the smoky heat of the night
on the deck
filled with beach balls
and rockers

Chairs in no order
so that feet can rest
on the banister
separating nature from home

A strange quiet
settles into the woods beyond
as the breeze from the north
nudges the trees ever so slightly
like a slow line dance

A scary screech
emerges from the distance
reminding us
the game of life
is breakfast for some
a nightcap for others

Something suddenly flies overhead
surely no bird
let's hope it does not perch

on the house wall

Time for some
night tea
steeped to perfection
for maximum relaxation
after the long day

A possum seems lost
in the distance
while a fox
seeks employ as
the local tour guide

Coyotes summon a family gathering
no guests allowed
except for those invited
by the hosts
for dinner

Best head inside
to do
what humans do best-
open the fridge door

———————————

David I Mayerhoff is an emerging literary writer, an
established scientific author and a Clinical Professor of
Psychiatry. Allpoetry.com/David_Mayerhoff

[Katharine L. Sparrow]

Black Water

This river,
where in summer, I used to wade,
searching for blue-claws
with my net —
It sparkled, then, with sunlight's jeweled spray.

Tonight it is black, dense and impenetrable,
though it moves, as always,
in ripples and little waves
that tumble into tiny ribbons of silver foam,
dimly lit by a cold, dispassionate moon.

Amazing—
that all this time,
since my childhood crabbing days,
it's been rolling on,
between these same shores, under the bridge,
through the channel
to join the vast, nameless sea.

Black water,
I need you to keep rolling on and on,
to carry strands of seaweed; brown and black and green,
like forgotten fragments of summers gone by—
to glint in the moonlight,
between the shores and under that bridge.

Black water,
keep on rolling and rolling—
rolling and remembering,
until you reach
the vast and nameless sea.

———————————

Katharine has been writing poetry since 2009 and has just finished the first draft her her first novel. She lives on Cape Cod, MA by the sea. Allpoetry.com/Ksparrow

[Stephen Hollins]

conversations with strangers

a brown bench stands in conversation with green grass
hanging pink and cream blossoms burst trees' branches
fuzzy bees dip silent diamond tongues into sunny flowers
mouths
spring airs scent of fruity apple blossom tickles the nose

female stranger pops by, an outsider, a park bench crasher
Baroque eyes look skywards her chest sighs, clouds track
full-bodied scarlet hair frames an olive face
skin tones of strawberry brushed onto cheekbones
dressed in a red pleated tartan skirt and black boots

my visitor takes a lifetime to show up
this blind match strikes the flint, a conversation ignites
first, it's the bodies settling into bodies, bench, space
she removes her purple leather gloves

I undo the top of my shirt tilting neck sideways
movement's pause, frames poems for openmouthed eyes
words fall out of lips filling the cup we drink from
hello, hi, have we met? no, sweet dog, thank you
pets, travel, clothes, food, life, the gold path

somehow I'm freer speaking to a stranger
then the people, I bump shoulders with daily
she sees me as my shadow does, just the way I am
not as an engineer fitting me into her shadows shapes

chatting faces smile under petals of dappled light
the treasure of clear distant mountains and tapping feet
orators of the new frontier flapping friendly flags
parrots muscular and nimble tongues talking turkey

sweet voices dance like rainbow-colored kite tails
we yak and laugh into the darkness of a watery womb
heartbeats feathered wings beating the amber sun
two adults lifted, pulling on a child's kite strings to fly again

---

I am loving writing poetry I live on Waiheke Island New
Zealand. I specialize in Improv for Theatre, Acting, Story
telling, Dance, Clown, Mime, Teaching, Building.
Allpoetry.com/Stephen_Hollins

[Bonnie-Jean Lee]

Pockets to Leaf

coins jingle jangle
coins jingle pockets

pockets that glove
pockets that warm

warm like summer
warm like treetops

treetops that reach
treetops that sing

sing taps of June
sing chords of rain

rain that glitters
rain that dances

dances in tempo
dances with hue

hue of Autumn
hue of apricot clay

clay sanded skies
clay of honied fire

fire that peaks
fire like sketches

sketches marigolds
sketches of bronze

bronze tiered hymns
bronze withered pale

pale as winter gaze
pale as snow twigs

twigs twining bare
twigs that shed

shed months past
shed bitter

bitter rinds of lemon
bitter frost

frost bitten windows
frost flowered hearts

hearts buried in earth
hearts waiting for April

April diamond stones
April larks of sunlight

sunlight dipped in Jupiter

sunlight painted with froth

froth against blue
froth skipping on waters

waters reflecting clouds
waters crashing to shores

shores lined with forests
shores of chestnut oak

oak bending olive leaf
oak in all seasons

seasons
leaf

_____

Bonnie-Jean Lee is a poet from southern N.H. I enjoy
photography, all genres of literature, art, and music.
Allpoetry.com/Skye_Darkholme

[Laurie Grommett]
A Mixed Musicale

The pandean pipes are playing in the breeze
and whistling a pitch from over the trees
as oboe da caccia crooning louise
when hard matchwood pieces tenor trapeze.

Then sky overhead toots by unaware
in blue basset oboe, bebop affair
for boogie is floating high in the air,
melodic, ragtime, a ripple flute flare.

While reeds of the river rustle ravine,
I hear jingle jangle of tambourine;
a riverboat landing flows in between
that takes me, first baroque, then upstream queen.

Laurie Grommett is a teacher that runs her own business; she believes learning is for life. Her poetry also spans the gamut of genres: humorous, fantastical, haunting, but it always comes from within. Allpoetry.com/L.G.

[Nathan Hill]

Efflorescent Lexicon

In nestled brake of arbored combe,
reposed on hoary bier.
Where silven webs snare nitid moon,
like precious lavalliere.

Limned by the garnet dahlia,
in endless syncope.
I sleep among the Moirai bloom,
as pawn of entropy.

With canopy as charnel house,
a chaplet girds my brow.
Of roses hued in maiden's blush,
implicit in their vow.

One latent hawthorn boutonniere,
adorns my static breast.
The sprig of buds evading burst,
awaits but one behest.

Corollas flit adrift each night,
along the chaparral.
To bathe within helenium,
and echo out a call.

Each petal weaves my tapestry,
a life in tacit prose.

Though if you hear but one of them,
pray, listen to the rose.

———————————

Michigan born and raised. Writing has been a coping
mechanism since childhood. I enjoy cooking, origami, and the
upper peninsula in my spare time. Allpoetry.com/Orpheus

[Paul Goetzinger]

South of Westport

Secluded coastal town
Swept by Pacific gales
A highway stretches south
Over foothills
Falling into the ocean
Amongst admiring pines
A towering lighthouse
Watches over rocky reefs
Warning distant ships
Away from watery graves
Sandy, windswept beaches
Shelter excited children
Making sand castles
Flying colorful kites
Blowing eastward
Searching for Crabs and Sand Dollars
Chasing Sea Gulls and Sand Pipers
Lofty waves
Crash on sand polished shores
Marooning lost driftwood
While rock jetties
Protect cowering boats
From remnants of tsunami's
Salmon charters
Chase wary customers
On moss covered boardwalks
While beyond high dunes

Hidden estuaries
Protect fallen trees
In backwater bays
Where Humpbacks
Expel air from blowholes
The road south ends
Only a path remains
Leading away
To distant capes

Paul Goetzinger is an educator and writer from Des Moines, Washington. He uses poetry to inspire and mentor his students. Allpoetry.com/Paul_Goetzinger

[Marilyn Griffin]

California Desert

Driving on the I-60
before following the curve of Banning
the topography dries up;
flinging sage and salvia
stirring the air sweet and cool

the mountain range
like a purple collar on a rocky basin
its ancient face cratered, wrinkled
closes bruised eyes
on a bright sun

around the bend near Nason
chugs a train
one car after anotheranother
passing California Pepper trees
planted to match the length
of each car

dropping into the valley
along the 62 to other desert cities-
a field of white windmill flowers
their propellers cartwheeling hypnotically
in the sky

and my dogs,
with Don Quixote courage

yip and watch them turn
with trembling noses
longing to stop, get out of the car
and wee in relief

I'd like to thank Kevin and everyone involved in putting these books together. It's such fun to see my poems in print! Thank you AP for a place to create!
Allpoetry.com/Greeningofautumn

[Stephen Hollins]

In the quiet of the night

in the quiet of the night
I slither like a Sandman slipping
between awake and sleep

that is when she appears
attending to a customer
part of her anesthetized

zooming in I track her face, eyes, lips, voice, hands
my fingers reach to brush her on the neck as I melt

a cube of ice in the burning sun
falling into a warm buttery gold liquid puddle
shimmering on red oak floorboards
of her rainbow-colored linen shop

people step into me, my golden syrup
sticks on the undersides of their feet
they post me by foot onto Berlin cobblestones

the underground, garden paths
steps, the same cafes, and shops
appear from when I visited her last

little is left pooled onto the floor
at days bell, her keys slip from tired fingers
landing into the last of me

she scoops me up in her keychain

riding with her a passenger on the bicycle
chill whistling wind dances with colored street lights
she slides me into her apartments door lock
smudges me onto the side of her cheek, hair

slips me between satin sheets
as the candle burns out
plumes of ghostly white smoke
thin into darkness

sleeping together
in the quiet of the night

I live on Waiheke Island New Zealand. I specialize in Improv for Theatre, Acting, Storytelling, Dance, Clown, Mime, Teaching, Building. Allpoetry.com/Stephen_Hollins

[Marilyn Griffin]

Gayle

In her contralto voice she sang;
a counterpoint solo
from an ancient hymn
teaching us how to hear the melody
from the harmony alone

Her skirt, a whorl of muted browns and yellows
the pattern hypnotic as she played.
A worn hymnal and a praise book,
side by side
amid sheet music lain
on the slick black lid.
Her long fingers skip elegantly
over the keys of the piano.

Flinging wide the lodge doors,
she'd lead us down to the river
bidding us:
listen
to the music of the earth

The reeds by the bank sway-
just the heavier tops
like muffled mallets pinging a xylophone
each one in a chromatic pitch

din
dan
dun

the voice of the river trilling
over the path of the song

at night, the campfire burped over thrown-on logs
sparking blue and green as we sat around it
singing the songs she taught us
in four part harmony.

The wind picked up,
our eyes tearing from the smoke
a gale to be reckoned with

She gave all of us a voice-
of kindness, acceptance, tolerance
her smiling eyes a reminder:
If no one else loved us, she did.
She did.

Her true harmony
the gentle melody

Loved ones who have passed still inspire me with their lives. I
will never forget them. They inhabit parts of my heart.
Allpoetry.com/Greeningofautumn

[Scott Waters]

Black Fireworks

the tall and tapering pine
bends like a cattail
in the grey wind

and what looks like
broken branches and pine cones
torn from the swaying top
turns out to be
as i walk closer
a vertical wheel of crows

cycling up from bobbing boughs
in some inscrutable order
so that every bird
has its turn
to hang like a dark kite
in the mistral
wings parrying the current

until with an expert
flick of feathers
each alights again
on the bucking
head-shaking pine

which knows nothing
of crows and their

black fireworks

but submits itself
with a creaking of joints
to the same superior power.

Scott Waters is a poet and songwriter living in Oakland, California, with his wife and son. He has published previously in The Pangolin Review, Ink in Thirds, A New Ulster, and other journals. Allpoetry.com/Scott_Waters

[Dale Cozart]

Black Widow

She waits,
eight black spindles joined at one end by a pivot, a compass.
Each pinpoint balanced at the intersections
of self-drawn polygons.
Legs jointed like the fingers of a skeleton,
deft, dexterous as a harpist.
Body in two sections with ample abdomen,
the African who carries the water jug on her head.
Or an Indian, the untouchable with her caste mark,
the microscopic grains dropping through the hourglass
like drops of blood.

Blind, she has the surrogate sense of a seismograph.
She would feel a disturbance in the web
were it only a thought.
Never mind she lives in a dark corner
as devoid of light as she is of personality,
she needs neither.
She does not look as the wrapped body of her cannibalized
mate
as at a gilt-framed photograph of the dearly departed.
The egg sac is not a silk-lined bassinet,
the hanging ornament
to all her future hopes and dreams.

She is absent of frontal lobes,
moralizing modifiers,

second thoughts.
An instrument of logic,
mate=food
sac=young,
syllogisms minus all prepositions,
additional excess cargo to be jettisoned
as the dried shells of devoured prey.
No welcome mats on the front step,
no settees in the parlor,
no cunning seductress with scarlet claws.
Only a modem waiting in the spaceless black.

I am a 60-year-old caretaker of my aunt. I've been writing
poetry since I was six, but only bean pursuing it more
seriously in the last two years. I live in Southern California.
Allpoetry.com/Dale_G._Cozart

[Peter Witt]

The Last Day

A failing red tractor pulled
the heavily loaded hay wagon
through the freshly mowed pasture
towards the faded barn

Wildflowers bloomed
in colored roadside ribbons
their bouquet smelled
like vanilla and lemonade

The farmer felt the weight
of decades of work falling heavy
on his stooped shoulders, displayed
sadly in his weathered face and hands

He was glad for this last load
of hay before the evening storm,
with its light show
draped the dry valley in rain

Today would end 63 years
of toil in the fields;
with the farm now sold
they would move to town

Gone would be treasured days
among strutting peacocks;

quiet time tending his carrots
lettuce, onions, yellow corn

He would always remember
the clanging bell calling him
to pause for a picnic lunch
under the aged willow

After lunch, he would sometimes
stretch out, rest his eyes
for just a few minutes before
taking up his work again

He weathered the seasons proudly
worked through cold, ice, snow
been buffeted by the streaking winds
survived the halting heat of summer

Now, he would talk grain prices
the weather, and local politics
with neighbors around a stove
at the county grain elevator

But most of all, he looked forward
to fishing the river with his grandson
sharing the boy's love of birds, squirrels,
his joy at a jumping fish, a passing rabbit

The boy would call him grandpa
he would call the boy junior

and welcome the remaining time
they would share

I am a retired university professor who took up poetry in
2018. Also write family history. Live in Texas, by chance,
with my community active wife and Keeshond, Quigley.
Allpoetry.com/Oakblue34

[Keith W Gorman]

Days of Locust

A dwarf-crested iris blooms by the brook;
hemlocks grown in shade minister the Sun.
The yellow corn, in rows, grows more from rain;
hot nights are a tempest around cool dawn.
She was leaving when you first heard the train.

A blue cataract covers the orphan eye;
ice appears glasslike on the overpass.
The green-speckled trout are sworn to be free;
Chinook salmon have all packed-up and fled
but the doors are still open by the marquee----

O' Pharaoh, can't you hear the locust sing?
around and round like a carnival swing----
Have Easter---- have buttered and honeyed tea;
let rough, rainy rivers run to the sea.

Savageheart is from Alcoa, Tennessee. Poetry is my escape
from working long, grueling hours in an auto parts factory. I
have a wonderful girlfriend, two cats and a pick-up. What
more do I need?   Allpoetry.com/Savageheart

[Stephen Hollins]

in the same breath

a man in green overalls straw hat and white gloves
glues colorful tiles onto a giant serpent creature
winding a path over the archway
of Casita Miro vineyard restaurant

people sprawled on red bean bags
scattered under olive trees
yellow and crimson roses dance against blue sky
leaves rustle and a bamboo wind chime chatters
in-between French and German accents
bathed in the hum of cicadas

we chink smiling wine glasses
diving into each others sparkling eyes
the warm airs lip whispers to me
this worlds pictured heartbeat
will never come back again

earth's novel flashing canvass of objects, bodies
garden, light, colors, and forces of nature
live and die at the click of a camera's shutter
as mother earth's sweet winds sing
'willkommen' and 'au revoir'
in the same breath

I am loving writing poetry I live on Waiheke Island New Zealand. I specialize in Improv for Theatre, Acting, Storytelling, Dance, Clown, Mime, Teaching, Building. Allpoetry.com/Stephen_Hollins

[Lisa F. Raines]

Our Lives and Times, Woke

We have such inadequate time,
to make much music or rhyme.

Yet we hope to mine
our own depths and breadths,

our debts, and deaths,
and finally what's left,

to elucidate and design
our lives, our times,

our rhythms,
and our rhymes.

—

We need some time to focus,
to understand the world that woke us;

demands from those
who provoke us,

defense from those
who choke us,

as we divine the locus of

our lives, our times,

our rhythms,
and our rhymes.

AlisRamie is from North Carolina, USA.
Interests include: philosophy, history, international relations,
poetry, art, design, jazz, funk, and some good old soul.
Allpoetry.com/AlisRamie

[Keith W. Gorman]

Together

Gazing inside the silvery-cold space
that surrounds us when we are older:
when we are rain-shaken
dream-delivered
dew-dispelled to a tiny island,
beating flames more taciturn than night.

Whispering along the wind-felled paths,
the frowns, the fences, the feathery worlds:
bracing, ballooning, breaking apart
so earth-less in a mouth of repair
that pointy stars are proud to snare
with their hot-red plasmas burning.

Fishing the outpost for an apple smile,
the sea, smooth and shimmering, while
on soft gray mornings mending barns,
how solid the heavy hands cling,
like new leaves turning deeper green;
like dogwoods drinking-down early Spring.

Dancing inside the silvery-cold space
that eludes us when we are younger:
when all the leaves and trees are bowing down
and the moon climbs over a shanty town –
Let us dance clear through the chestnut blight,

the caves, the sands and the starry night.

———————————

Savageheart is from Eastern Tennessee. Poetry is an escape from factory work, and I also play classical guitar. Allpoetry.com/Savageheart

[Marilyn Griffin]

Strings of Yucca Valley

Looking up the hill to the east
past the saguaro cactus
behind the manzanita tree
trickles a string of traffic lights

desert mountains
with elephantine boulders teetering
on the edge of falling
where the lavender cliffs highlight
strings of rocks

sweet cool air
buffets the sheets hung horizontally
waving; a string of damp laundry

a little cotton tail scampers
there, you see it?
behind the silvered diamonds of
chain-link
nope, he's gone

while I sing a goodbye,
you stick your hand out waving
and drive away to join
the string of red lights
fading back up the Yucca hill
into the matched hot horizon

thank you AP for hearing my small voice in such a huge world! I love writing for you and I am so grateful to all the poetfriends I've made on here who've helped me with my poetry. Blessings! Allpoetry.com/Greeningofautumn

[Lisa F. Raines]

Gerrymandering

Using a pencil

You erase our history

Deliberately

Leaving us nothing

You rewrite our history

Politically

AlisRamie is from North Carolina, USA.
Interests include: philosophy, history, international relations,
poetry, art, design, jazz, funk, and some good old soul.
Allpoetry.com/AlisRamie

[Stephen Hollins]

the architect's colorful belly

I step into the Fisherman's five-star restaurant
falling inside the architect's colorful belly
sitting with pen in hand, coffee flaring nostrils
muses feathered quilled horses
cribbing at the starters gate

letters, commas, semicolons
congregate the canvas of my tight skin
waiting for the camps bugle to call

short pearly light flashes
skies towering lighthouse floods
blinds the brain shortly to unlock
sweet rivers flowers of honeyed sap
nine thousand gold bee's wings humming

elixir's fire fuels this poem's juices
illuminating ink warriors quills
lightning bolts and they're racing
text scrambling over text

arranging grouping arguing
words filling with wind
some popping colored balloons
chaos assembled to order
march a black-inked assault
onto the white virgin page

for what vein may you ask
do this poet's literary battles take place?

to write a poem to you, my stranger
yes you
this crystallized woven silk cocoon
metamorphosing onto the cream

two of us flying tandem
strapped to my back
falling off this page into eyes
stepping in
in- to- me- you -see

that I treasure you, my stranger
more than both of us can tell

pause

for a dark night's starry silence
that I can hear inks silent text
drop and drip into my strangers well
a heartbeating chest for polished jewels

we may not meet that's true
death may ring her copper bell
to lay me still in the hornets bed

black inks butterfly wings to sing

something, some little trinket
outside this poet's skulled head

I am loving writing poetry I live on Waiheke Island New Zealand. I specialize in Improv, physical theatre, storytelling, clown doctor, teaching adults the art of play and building Allpoetry.com/Stephen_Hollins

[Kim Van Breda]

libretto's sash sung

tiny yellow beads
lay scattered crowding
these afterthoughts. What
once were hobbies, cost

a lewd quack rampant,
agoraphobic
boards. Lavish hair strands,
abandoned braided shores

proudly sprung highs
blue canopy sighs
dark lanterns paused
omniscience, brave
pointless valuables

stubbed toe, pear swear bombs,
encroaching insects
distributing coiled
bedspreads, silk spun puns

libretto's sash sung
high-pitched off quickened
rays, confused life taxed
father-land sitcoms

With a distinctive contemporary abstract style my recent collection of literacy pieces range across a broad spectrum from, human experiences, short poems and prose to mythical themes. Allpoetry.com/Mermaid

[Marta Green]

The Cicada Musician

growing Cicada grubs
eating the delectable root juices
living underground for thirteen years until these large insects
climb out of rain soaked mud for a single week

large green insects that have big yellow eyes
shed their skin leaving an exact replica
of its former body, a brown, crunchy shell
hanging on trees, fence posts and walls

listening to the musical buzz and vibrations
the forests is alive with life
summer is just beginning
where they can be heard like a chamber of music

it is soothing to hear these intriguing insects
mid morning, through the heat of the afternoon,
into the quiet as night falls asleep,
with windows open listening to the symphony

I have been married to my best friend for 10 years who makes
me laugh to no end. My passions are family, animals,
especially writing, reading and art!
Allpoetry.com/Marta_Green

[Sharon Leigh]

Neptune on a Wednesday

I meet him where the salt marsh
sucks the earth, a silver day
of rain, no tourists. We are pale
against the swaying sawgrass, his eyes

a riptide, pulling: danger for the swimmer,
caution. What is this quality of light?
We speak of boats, or clamming, small talk
swept away on stinging winds. His smile

chapped, brine and self assurance, rows
of white against the beard, chamois skin.
Where is the trident, the coral crown?
Storms pile at his fair isle shoulder,
broad as the east horizon.

Sharon Leigh has loved language since childhood. Her work
often centers around family, parenting, and women's issues.
She lives in Michigan with two sons, one daughter and a
geriatric parakeet. Allpoetry.com/Sharon_Leigh

[Stuart Williamson]

Intrepid Spaceman.

Dark brown paisley silk bandanna
Corners carefully tied with twine
A harness fit for plastic spacemen
Catapulted to the skies

The astronaut flew even higher
Past the point of safe return
Way beneath the plastic space-boots
The boy ran on through kale and fern

Over hedges, gateposts, fences
Tripping often, falling down
"Earth to Spaceman, losing contact"
Space to Earthman, not a sound

The spaceman now flew ever skyward
Just a spec, much smaller now
The boy fell back amongst the cornstalks
Tired and sad, yet proud somehow.

Just like every passing moment
Full of strife and happiness
Things forgotten, much remembered
Quite a ride, supremely blessed.

I was born in the NE of Yorkshire, iron ore mining country. I have been a professional sculptor for 30 years, and a painter before that, but in only recent years turned to poetry for expression. Allpoetry.com/SculptorPoet

[Stephen Hollins]
India No Turning Back

cars, bikes, rickshaws, trucks, and buses
a thousand shades of honking horns
metal and rubber filling all the gaps
merging like spaghetti on hot tarmac

every vehicle a carnival rally driver
motorbike stacked with a family of four
push bike piled high in polystyrene boxes
cars overtaking, weaving in and out

final race flag waving, chassis missing
a collision by inches, shoulders
bumping shoulders in the back seat

colorful flashes of sarees, jewelry, fruit
copper dishes, leather bags, umbrellas
gripping smoke of barbequed meat
followed by incense and black diesel fumes

businessmen, beggars, soldiers, tourists
farmers, construction workers, and students
little colored logo people slotting into life's stream

a slim mid-road strip offers grassing for three horses
and two cows, a black bull lies in the middle of the street
he completely ignores the barrage of horns, forcing
traffic to skirt around him as his tail flaps fly

Hindu spiritual guru jiggles on the dashboard
drivers hand on the steering wheel
the other on the horn and his iPhone
tooting and swearing, his feet jive from

break to the accelerator as he turns up the
radio belting out Bollywood's latest gold hit
a fork-tailed kite flies above in the clear space
looking down at swarming metal maggots

a kaleidoscope of color, people, sound, smells
caous, aliveness, spirituality, poverty and wealth
ejaculating life onto arterial streets and highways
no turning back

———————————————

I am loving writing poetry I live on Waiheke Island New
Zealand. I specialize in Improv for Theatre, Acting,
Storytelling, Dance, Clown, Mime, Teaching, Building.
Allpoetry.com/Stephen_Hollins

[Nancy E. Jackson]

An Oceanside Tale

Lying beside the ocean's edge
I blearily stare into the horizon
while waves curl and twist,
wash over sand and rocks,
dissolve into foam then
retreat to dance again.

I drift into a trance.

In my most resplendent guise,
as if this were a daily occurrence,
I saunter steadily across the top
of white-ribboned waves
as they break and crash
over the larger cliff faces.

Without warning, a large creature
with steel-trap jaws
and needlepoint sharp teeth
pull me under again and again
with no chance of release
from an indefatigable grip.

Through the misty haze,
hovering above the waterline,
I hear a wailing noise so piercing,
so guttural and full of anguish

I ache even more
to flee the beast below.

The heartrending sound calling from the mist
was rising from deep within
as a searing pain pulsed throughout my body,
for the frenzied beast had gnawed me in two -
bright crimson cells were splaying
over the sea-foam green of the ocean.

I awoke searching for blood, ready to die.

Though fully present
the inexpressible agony remained,
and with temples throbbing and breathing labored
I raised my head and my hands
and cried out with inconsolable explosions
to the One who hears my pleas -

My brother is dead.

———————————————

Nancy grew up on a peninsula by calm and thrashing waters.
She lives near foothills of blue smoke; her yards are havens
for wild birds. Poetry gives voice to the world inside and
outside of her. Allpoetry.com/Nancy_daisygirl

[Gopal K Maharjan]

Nepal!

Wrapped with silver and standing tall
based on the height of fully green hilltop
even the marble might feel jealous with this rock
sun's first ray glows in it, peoples' treasure and luck
a symbol of world's adventurous quest
one and only the Mount Everest

Thousands of big and small cascades
flowing down curtain of diamonds, a scenic heartfelt
more than half a thousand of species of butterflies
during the mid October, flying kites in the sky
various of endangered animals and birds
unique creation of nature blessed by love

Rivers with crystallized water, happy trees with monsoon's
showers
densely and wildly blooming rhododendrons-rose flowers
harvesting of rice, wheat, corn and other crops
innocent and guest friendly localities of cities and suburbs
traditionally dressed beautiful men and women
In the streets, on the hay straws' mattresses, drying grains

Everywhere temples of gods and goddesses
superb architectural monuments invoking for caress
plenty of Buddhists' stupas and monasteries
almost everyday, carnivals' and festivals' series

fiesta of ladies, lights, and colors, to name the few
sing, dance, and eat until the morning's dew

Somethings are not told, these are supposed to be felt. When I
think I am strong enough to tell about myself, I will be present
myself there to represent you. Thank you.
Allpoetry.com/Gkmaharjan

[Gene Simia]

Father of Our Country

It was on or about 1732,
on Pope's Creek Farm, his birth was due.
The world hadn't seen such a child ordained,
to give our country, new life obtained.

At the age of twenty one,
he made major in the Virginia sun.
Commanding a militia at twenty two,
surrendering once, while the French subdued.

Accepting the terms at Necessity Fort,
an admission to the death of a diplomat sort.
With French and Indian neighboring kin,
a terrifying war was soon to begin.

It was in the year of 1755,
this unflinching man had again survived.
Braddock's men counted thirteen hundred,
nearly destroyed, as the French and allies thundered.

He was seen bringing Braddock out from the field,
an American hero, had just been sealed.
His fame spread wide throughout the land,
defying death, with life in hand.

A victory claimed by the British won,
his life's work had just begun.

Accepting the hand of a widow's call,
begins a new life as treasure's befall.

His marriage in the year of '59,
brought fortune, land, with servants behind.
With adoption of children from his cherished wife,
Patsy and Jacky completed his life.

As ambition would have it, he would continue to add,
twenty-three thousand acres a land bounty he had.
This gentleman planter, one of the elite,
had his sights on the legislature sure to replete.

As pressure would mount from the British at hand,
the Stamp and Townsend Acts would tax our land.
In 69' our hero introduced,
a boycott on what the British produced.

A revolution of sorts had begun to surge,
soon Lexington and Concord would begin to urge.
Our leader was chosen as commander in chief,
no one before him could enhance their belief.

Effectively training his scattered troops,
taking the indigent into strengthened groups.
With help from the French, their navies at hand,
gave hope independence would be in our land.

As Yorktown had sealed the win by the French,
our troops had come forth from the field and the trench.
Washington lauded like no other before,

opening the future, through yet another door.

Leaving Virginia for this inaugural place,
New York City was to set the pace.
This temporary capital in 1789,
gave birth to our first president, sentiments benign.

Gene Simia makes his home in Munroe Falls, Ohio, along
with his wife Yvonne Simia. He is also a pianist,
percussionist and singer/songwriter. Yvonne writes children's
books and teaches art. Allpoetry.com/William_Pencraft

[Jim Voell]

Andy

The aging fisherman waits
On the concrete jetty
His back to the scrub pine
The hardwood bottom flatland
His face to the wind
Watching approaching waves
Break softly over themselves,
Memories in motion,
Seaborne benedictions.

The frigid asphalt strip
A meandering black
Barrier along the Gulf coast
Is flanked by molded dragons
Covered with blazing colors
Whitened skulls, fierce faces
Silent rampaging predators.
Plastic sentinels
Prowl the cold, guard the shore,
Silently challenge the deep.
Lurking swimming nightmares,
Great white sharks, whales
Lusting just offshore
Awaiting the trident mullet.

Life's fire fades quickly
Weary pilgrim.

Summer's heat yields
As artic fronts sweep southward.
All that remains are the constant waves
Gently beckoning at your feet.

This aged angler, the potato King
Shifts slightly on his jetty throne,
His loyal companion, his royal valet,
His ever alert poodle, nearby
Patient on a weather worn leather leash.

The images wash in on flood tide
Heaving waves,
Our sun seeking Canadian Snowbird
Although slightly out of his element
In the briny shallows, yet
Totally in harmony with
Years of lived moments
Reappearing in memories
Before his searching aging eyes.
Multitudes of thrashing pike
Northern, walleye, whitefish,
Dancing brilliance of northern lights,
Flashing razor sharp filet knives,
Disappearing Y bones,
Crackling shore fires,
Warm cabins at dusk,
Crystalline northern lights,
Ontario stars,
Portages and blueberries,
Tipsy Indians, angling tourists.

Images emerge
From lost horizons,
Fade in the mist

The lakes, sea, fishermen, bounty,
Supplications at the water's edge,
All become one and gently beckon

The old man rests at the lone end
Of his seaside jetty
Having fished his thousand lakes
Awaits his meeting
His Divine Fisherman
Deep in star studded night
When the crystal sands are darkened
When the last tidal reach
Recovering the last planetary memory
Ebbs back
Returning to moonlit glowing sea.

Married 60 years this June 20. Started writing poetry about
50+ years ago. A way of recording my passing life. Serves as
a kind of memoir of my life as a confused pilgrim,
Allpoetry.com/Ipmpitc5

[Carl Wayne Jent]

Amalfi, the Place for Me

As we flew into Amalfi, past over the Gulf of Salerno
could see its beauty at the foot of Monte Cerreto
laying so lovely at the bottom of the dramatic cliffs
smelt the fresh sea air with a couple of whiffs.

Staying at the converted monastery named Luna Convento
with so much to see, made a plan on the places to go
hotel was exquisite with decorative spacious rooms
everywhere we went there was fragrant lush blooms.

Seaside quaint, citizens so polite, always saying please
rumored that city was built by the Roman God, Hercules
after making it the burial site of his adoring wife, Melphe
city dates back before the dark ages, about the 4th century.

Took bus on the fabled route to artsy city of Positano
ventured over to crafts on winding streets of Sorrento
discovered Isle of Capri was only a ferry ride away
decide to put that destination off till another day.

Tomorrow, plan on visiting Pompeii and Mount Vesuvius
trip should be fun, take a while on the small tourist bus
Of all the places I've been, there's a place, love the most
where air is clean, sea is shimmering, the Amalfi Coast.

The poems I write, I write for comfort. To read and ponder life's journey and feel a little better about my existence. I believe life is wonderful and Earth a place to behold. Allpoetry.com/Waynejent

[Stephen Hollins]

rocketing dancers into space

sunsets breeze floats orange silk curtains through windows
in Gabrielle Roths 5 rhythms gestalt therapy spaceship
dancers bodies move in waves and patterns
my naked feet slide onto a sprung wooden floor

the silent dancer is the terrains vehicle, steering me
swirling to straight and spiral painted strokes
facing the call of voices yawning deep inside

with my eyes closed tongues multiply on my skin
taste buds licking the sweet airs fragrance

fingers wrists forearms elbows shoulders
cut through the air a shining blade
slicing into a musicians wedding cake

colorful people stand, candles on cream icing
their wax bodies dripping into golden maple floor

locomoting scarlet and yellow scarf's flap
my body leaping into abstract gymnastics
birthing novel choreographic sketches
moving pictures feast upon gold banquet tables
of the Romans to a Japanese ninja warrior

twists and twirls, I fall in and out of the boards
elbows, knees, heels, and toes skipping

to the percussive beat of bass and drum

multi-colorful music builds chaos that fires
less visited corridors within my castle walls
baiting and luring me to lose myself
journey the labyrinth of new pathways

gestures blossomed into dancing chords
musical limbs fly off the page
sounds heartbeat rockets
dancers into space

I live on Waiheke Island New Zealand. I specialize in Improv for Theatre, Acting, Storytelling, Dance, Clown, Mime, Teaching, Building. Allpoetry.com/Stephen_Hollins

[Jonathan Moya]

Nun Sense

Sister Dorothea would whack my knuckles
with the flat edge of a desk ruler
trying to knock some nun sense into me
every five times I messed up on fractions.

She had that well lived-in roundness
the faithful get after hard years
of serving Christ in the smallest
crosses of existence.

From the back she resembled
a Magellanic penguin waddling
the beach of Magdalena Island,
and diving into the Argentine waves.

During recess she and the other sisters,
a raft of congregants, would assemble
in the gymnasium and mercilessly beat us
with their basketball moves.

Her Spanish was not the typical
Spanglish of the Miami Cuban young,
but that native exotic gaucho brio
that sounded incomprehensively French.

Che Guevara had once motorcycle to
Parana, her pueblo del corazón,

kilometers from his own beloved Rosario,
stopping for a fit of asthmatic whimsy.

She gave him some water to soothe his cough
and in his thanks she saw and heard Jesus.
He turned left and embraced la revolución.
She went right into el Papa's arms.

Their affinity for the poor children
was the road they trod,
the journey they traveled,
the smile they shared.

That shared grin was as wide
as the continent and the Milk Way,
yet as contained as the Christ icon
that elevated her every breath.

Only la guerra could erase la sonrisa.
Che would often stop mid onslaught,
Dorothea imagined, to cry for a
martyred child cradled in his arms.

That sonrisa compartida would dissolve
into defiance when the Death Squads arrived
clamoring for more los desaparecidos
who desired only sanitized water, a clean word.

They ordered her to move. She refused.
When they demanded again, she whacked
the capitan on the knuckles with a

Monkey Puzzle branch a child had gifted her.

The capitan tore her habit down the center
and ordered his men to defile her ten times.
He demanded half the innocents slaughtered,
their bodies carried out for the caracaras delight.

El Papa moved Dorothea to a safe healing place
where in time she could feel the sun again,
hear Jesus call her to protect the innocent
one more time and forever.

The other sisters on the pick-up BB squad
all shared the same call and delighted in
the fierce protection of their wards.
They never challenged charging or traveling violations.

For these niños y niñas, me among them,
it was a time for them to heal, to learn to
bend in the wayward movement of the light,
the soft tough love tap of ruler to flesh.

I am a retired shopkeeper and former Walt Disney World cast
member who lives to write about movies and some poetry.
Allpoetry.com/Jonathan_Moya

[Mike F. Gombas Sr.]

The Body

The yellow orb true to its appointed ark,
slipped beneath a tapestry of emerald green.
Midnight's stealthy fingers heralded the coming dark,
changing the world of color into the drab unseen.

The foaming confluence of icy flows,
Freed from confining walls of stone,
Deposited bits and pieces of debris in the shallows,
Boulders drift wood and bleached white bone.

Among the tangled mess of soggy refuse,
in a tiny cove obscured by chaotic shades of gray,
A listless form was draped over a gently swaying spruce,
barely discernible amid the piled up disarray.

Mike Gombas Sr. is a retired Navy Chief Petty Officer. Mr. Gombas is married to his lovely wife Phyllis and they have two adult children Tara and Mike Jr. Allpoetry.com/Matroz

[Arlice W Davenport]

Never Be Afraid of the Serious Life

"I like the bullfights," the Belgian tourist said,
"whenever the bull wins."
"Which is never," I said. "Yes."

I thought of Hemingway and the horses.
Look away, look away.
In the *corrida*, no one wins. No one ever wins.

Not the bull, of course, dragged across the sand,
to be drawn and quartered.
No hunt, no chase. Maddening circle of death.

Not the matador, bloody ear in hand,
parading to a mob's applause,
praised for the piercing jabs of
banderilleros and *picadors*, workmen
who steal his easy conscience.

No one ever wins; still let us
embrace the color of Spain: black.
Black holds against the white of atonement.
Black holds against the memory of betrayal.
Black holds against repetition, initiation, brutality.

At five in the afternoon, Ignacio Sanchez Mejias died,
gored by a bull's heavyweight boxer's horns.
A wound in the thigh, a pool of blood, gangrene,

the cold stone of death. Lorca's lament:

Oh white walls of Spain!
Ah black bull of sorrow!
Oh hard blood of Igancio!
Oh nightingale of his veins!
No, I do not want to see it.

Look away, look away.
In the *corrida*, no one wins. No one ever win

*   *   *

Never be afraid of the serious life.
Embrace the black of Spain. It holds against all art.
An aging matador dies in the sand.
A martyred poet pens his lament.
An American painter spills massive amounts of black paint.
A Spanish poet writes an elegy to Ignacio,
then a paean to the painter:

Motherwell's black
profound compact entered into with night
Black of this land of eternal black
Oh black wall of Spain!
Still black airless obituaries
Pain of black concentrated anguish

Listen to the black of Alberti: *Call off your bulls....*
Turn back and brace for that avalanche, the scarlet
stampede of the bulls.

No one wins. No one ever wins.

* * *

Embrace the black, the Spanish black. It holds back
the fury of imagination.

Embrace the black, the Spanish black. It holds back
the tide of violence.

Embrace the black, the Spanish black. It holds back
the desolation of exile.

Embrace the black, the Spanish black. It holds back
the failure of nerve.

Embrace the black, the Spanish black. It holds back
the profundity of love.

Embrace the black, the Spanish black. It holds back
the precision of perception.

Embrace the black, the Spanish black. It holds back
the architecture of mind.

Embrace the black, the Spanish black. It holds back
the dream of sol y sombra.

Embrace the black, the Spanish black. It holds back
the black of Alberti's "five senses
blackened:

black sight
and black sound,
black smell
and black taste; and the painter's black,
black to the touch."

Embrace the black, the Spanish black. It holds back
the black song of the earth.
Embrace the black, the Spanish black. It holds back
the blackened black of black death.
Embrace the black, the Spanish black. It holds back
the black hollows of the black *corrida*.

*   *   *

"I like the bullfights," the Belgian tourist said,
"whenever the bull wins."
"Which is never," I said. "Yes."

In the *corrida*, no one wins. No one ever wins.
Never be afraid of the serious life.
Embrace the black, the Spanish black.
Then look away, look away. Always look away.

This poem contains many of my interests when it was written:
the poetry of Lorca, paintings of Motherwell, allure of Spain,
Hemingway, the ethics of bullfighting, and, of course, the
Spanish black. Allpoetry.com/arliced

[Alwyn Barddylbach]

Dream of the East

I dreamt of earth in all her incidental beauty,
incarnate birth of love and fate, a temple rose,
I learnt her orient pleasures, whims and curses,
mocking moons whenever an east wind blows.

In the Gobi desert rain her flower opens,
in glassy mountain streams river giants grow,
in terrace fields and wild bamboo woodland,
in silk, sand and rock the tao sojourn flow.

Gunpowder, papyrus, chess and porcelain,
wooden junks and sails upon her ocean bob and fro,
pagoda palaces of iron, fire, gold and clay
ordained in dragon's jade wherever they would go.

Below forbidden city walls and ancient kingdoms,
terracotta shadows baking in the sun,
I learnt her orient pleasures, spice and curses,
mocking moons whenever an east wind blows.

I dreamt of Shangri-La in all her transcendental beauty,
a stony lamasery concealed in lotus clouds,
I wandered east as far as earth might take me,
upon my merchant book of maps and marvels browse.

Song of a traveller - Marco Polo was first to leave a detailed chronicle of his travels in the far east (c.1300). I am just a Londoner recounting mine from where the sun rises - AB 2018. Allpoetry.com/Barddylbach

[Eric Grady]

Upon the Discovery of a Suicide

a fist driven relentlessly deep,
the herculean bicep curls into your chest,

whistling away any air left in the lungs
as if a white-hot tea kettle losing steam,

violently thrashing a palpitating heart, beat upon
unnaturally by drunk satirical jazz percussionists,

words become a delusory semblance of syntax
and shrieks as your throat implodes,

forearm and elbow now a crashing bony tide
against the hull of that forever sunken heart,

paralysis as the brain stem, popped and racked,
severs communication below the neck,

vertebrae splinter between the knuckled
blow and the weight of the moment,

momentum slows but not before reaching reason,
fingers slowly knead the brain,

twisting as an industrial impeller through the thoughts
that bind the bricks of your mind,

in the ensuing insanity, there is nothing to take hold,
no red button, no safety switch or plug to pull,

it is powered by the day's reservoir
of carbohydrates, sugar and adrenaline,

not ceasing until it has consumed it all,
leaving behind a stumbling, cored-out slough

———————————————

Eric began writing poetry on Dec 13, 2018 to process
emotions spilled post-discovery of his Mother's suicide. He
will continue improving his poetry through study, writing, and
self-discovery. Allpoetry.com/Usurp

[Marta Green]

Day Dreaming

lost in thought, visions of what is to come
emerald isle with light green grasses
winds that blow long hair into our faces
the air is clean and pristine

walking in the rocky hills, warmed by movement and sunlight
as we sit down to eat a lunch brought in a basket
sandwiches with ham and cheese slices
spotted dick pudding for desert

apple cider to quench my thirst
the walk continues on to the old mansion
where it is dark and damp
on to the kitchen to clean up

we go upstairs on the winding staircase
to lie in bed and rest from the exertion of the exercise
while asleep, I dream of the moors
muddy and boggy, boots being suctioned in.

I have been married to my best friend for 10 years who makes
me laugh to no end. My passions are family, animals,
especially writing, reading and art!
Allpoetry.com/Marta_Green

[Stephen Hollins]

land of the long white cloud

New Zealand is the land of the long white cloud
crafted with the surreal beauty of a Peter Jackson movie set
travelers boast treasures of earth staggering wonders
packed into a small country of snow-capped peaks
rainforests, deserts, coastal glaciers
icy fiords, fish-filled rivers, and waterfalls

carrying my landscape camera I fly from north to south
capturing an ocean of country, fauna, and culture
that most of its inhabitants have not explored

dawns yellow sunbeams illuminate champagne bubbles
swirling in turquoise tides on the east coast beaches
boiling plopping mud pools serve the morning's porridge
for Ruaumoko, the god of volcanoes and earthquakes

hissing geysers erupt to a fierce Maori haka war dance
violent foot-stamping, rhythmic body slapping
wide-eyed Pukana tongue stretching and baring teeth
tattooed chins ink pride, strength, and unity

vast snow-peaked mountains vaulting in the distance
my helicopters silver wings lift open-mouthed tourists
over white glaciers, ice walls, and hungry crevices

soft rolling green hills peppered with sheep and bush
silent kiwi birds hide as the cheeky colorful kea prance

southern coasts shy hector's dolphin makes way
to the exuberant hooker's sea lion

on Coromandel beach, a shovel digs a hole in the sand
geothermal hot water rises to dance naked legs
mingling with the cold ocean waves
a glass of Mudbrick's velvety red melts delirious tastebuds
as the tide rolls in and out at the last stop of the day

white and purple lavender flowers
flood my wooden cottage balcony
green lawn stretches to my island home
amongst the manuka trees at Okoka bay

red flowering flax-bush flag the blue and green Tui bird
his white throat tufts and bronze iridescent sheen
mark this New Zealander, a warrior of the sky

the tide makes its way skipping up the salty mud flats
birds make last calls

triumphant sun scrapes her lips over a calm turquoise sea
sunrays fanned arms of amber and gold clouds
bid the sun adieu

as I come home to myself
I hang up work
for another day

I am loving writing poetry I live on Waiheke Island New Zealand. I specialize in Improv for Theatre, Acting, Storytelling, Dance, Clown, Mime, Teaching, Building. Allpoetry.com/Stephen_Hollins

[Jacob Frederick]

The Dialogue of a Desperate Man

In some black backwater alley
a man lights his last cigarette.
Orange tip reflects
in garbage water puddles
like ancient Aramaic lights
that shewn upon better men.
Then a rat scurries across,
disrupting the latticework
impressed in the pitch.

A man stands like Hazael,
suffocator of kings
and ender of stories,
though only looking
to end his own.

A man converses with Elisha.
how will it end?
With the hoofbeats of a hundred horses
throbbing in my chest?
Will my own throat be made a delta,
spewing forth sea foam
and sputtering words for deaf ears?
Am I to be made a footnote in a greater book
as all kings will one day be?
Is my life to be etched upon the base
of a monument to greater rulers?

Elisha stands
a paramount of perpetuity.
donned in purple robes
that bespeak of palaces beyond
what normal men may see,

and as he stands before Hazael
king of the Aramaeans of old
the wise man proclaims

"Go home, you're drunk"

Speaking expresses ideas
Music expresses passion
Poetry expresses both

I believe that it can change the world
Allpoetry.com/Dizzy_Lemons

[Vidushi Upadhyay]

The Indian Rains

Nebulous day yet propitious to all.
After four months of suffering the rude sun,
witnessing unusual burning walls.

The houses in the lane are covered by felicitous birds.
Grandiloquent trees not willing to undress the reeking cover,
showering the grouped weeds playing under their shade.

Appears as a live painting colored in green and gray,
hypnotic in its natural ways.

Not only nature;
mother in the kitchen, priest in the temple
and farmers on the field,
thank the roaring clouds in songs of praise.

Creeks overjoyed and spilling their colors all around,
children dancing and searching their water-bed playground,
all set with their paper boats.
Grand-mothers recalling their encounters with happy rains.

There comes the most anticipated season in India.
Floods making the news, blocked roads declaring a day off.
Troubles a bit but we enjoy all that rain brings.

Vidushi is from Mumbai, India. To me, poetry is the best way to express myself.I am still under learning and wish if I can be a novelist some day :) Allpoetry.com/Vidushi

[David I Mayerhoff]

Secret Agent

Looking this way and that
he walks across the street
a mask of stealth
like the chameleon deploys its skin

Vultures squawk with tongues of alarm
as he swerves into the domain of the enemy
dressed like a lost friend

Fingers turning the pages in his pocket
searching for the contact
that is not listed
on a street that is not known
in a land of silver tongue
and quiet death

Boys kicking soccer balls
as if the battle
is already joined

Passers-by are all threats
in this arena of cat and mouse
nerves doing a reset
as a pulse escalates
seeing the bulge in another's coat

Weapon or lunch,

gloves or a cap
he must choose quickly
as life of the spy hangs in the balance

A strange noise around the bend
a horn honking out of place
the poised shopper dropping her bags
a beggar soliciting where none are allowed

Mist seeps over the distant mountain
with all species of bird
hiding within

The agent cracks a smile of recognition
as he puts his head down
to blend in
with the tapestry of the surround

David I Mayerhoff is an emerging literary writer, an
established scientific author, and a Clinical Professor of
Psychiatry Allpoetry.com/David_Mayerhoff

[Peter Witt]

Black and White

Venus lifts delicate slices
of orange to her painted lips
and sighs as each drop
runs down her chin

Black hair drapes
across her pale neck
falling down her beckoning back
silky tips almost reaching
her wispy waist

Nestling against her feet
a black cat stretches,
nails scratch the rug,
then reaches upward
to lick with rough tongue
the gently extended hand
of his mistress
before curling into
a purring ball at her feet

The day blackens
lightning flashes in the distance
storm clouds gather
rain drops stain tilled earth
in the spring garden

Sipping black coffee,
her spirit swiftly darkens
with the nearing sound of thunder
the staccato rhythm of spattering rain
increases, along with her breathing

Without warning the cat
is gone, slithering away
to a cold black space
beneath the bed

Alone, our black-haired Venus
bends her head in meditation
allowing her mind to go white
safety sought in the cosmos

Suddenly she wakes
beneath white sheets
with the last sliver
of a milky moon
shining through her window

Dressed in her egg shell colored robe
she pets an alabaster cat
notices the blanket of freshly fallen snow
resumes her pale existence

––––––––––––––––––––

Peter Witt is a retired university professor. He writes family
history, collects Inuit art, travels to iconic places, and loves
his allpoetry.com experiences. Allpoetry.com/Oakblue34

[Stephen Hollins]
Cold Nordic Waters

Cold waters anchor a fisherman's hungry heartbeat
Ocean channels feed flocks of soaring seagulls
Larval whitefish nets a cool transparent camouflage
Dutch harbor nourishes deep tumbling darkness

Noordwijk's refrigerated enthusiasm kitesurfs rainbows
Origami migrating seabirds silhouetted on the gold horizon
Remainders claw back a diet of the suns orange
Daredevil water bathers fire up hot blood in blue veins
Indigenous wildflowers sleep in spikey grass dunes
Colorful blo-karting sails cut and laugh the chill breeze

Watercolor brushes paint a canvas on the cream bank
Anadromous whitefish refund from seas spawn
Transparent veils cloak pinprick crystal eyes
Earth's sandy edges kiss a salty sea-foam song
Rhetorical sleights rime in the cloud of a March foghorn
Seaside skiing on the soft snow of Nordic beaches

An acrostic. I am loving writing poetry. I live on Waiheke
Island, New Zealand. I specialize in Improv for Theatre,
Acting, Storytelling, Dance, Clown, Mime, Teaching,
Building. Allpoetry.com/Stephen_Hollins

[Sally M. Clark]

from cave to Tunnel

laboriously scrawled
by an isolated
stone-faced
sedentary
stagnant
dismal
hollow shell
long since gone
human life
in overdrive
survival mode
trappings
musty
endless
dead-end
dungeon

to

Self-determined
iron will
bruised
battered
scarred and cracked,
a human being
with an unbreakable spirit.

She chooses
to stand
shoulders erect
head held high
threshold
uncharted
unkempt
in this seemingly endless
Tunnel.

Fiery eyes
bore holes
that snake
through the black
luminescence
emanates
Holy Trinity
handmade hope
unflagging faith
indefatigable fortitude.

She stands
at the threshold

blood-thirsty glass shards
bile orange
tetanus-infected
rust-riddled
metal shrapnel.

Inch by inch,

by a hair's breadth,
evades
the front line
a smattering
serrated
shark-tooth crags
buckled concrete.

Malevolent
pitfalls
peppered
path

She walks
always forward
remote
minuscule
slice
effulgent splendor
valiant
obscure
abstraction.

An existential impetus
singular force
propels
forward
starving
for sunlight.

Promise

transcendence
ethereal exeunt
cast-off
caustic
comedy of errors

a life worth living

She stumbles
falters
slips
falls
chokes
metallic tang
freshly oxygenated blood.

Untangling limbs
she shudders
rips the eight-legged
coarse-haired
elephantine creature
from knotted
sweat-drenched
curls.

Swipes furiously
claws
loathsome
sticky strings
adhered to
dirt-smeared

blood-stained
tear-streaked
sunken cheeks.

She stands
and walks.

Clasping clammy
trembling hands
white-knuckled
desperation
"God, grant me the serenity
to accept
the things I cannot change
the courage
to change the things I can
and the wisdom
to know the difference."

She walks
always forward

refusing
to dart
red-rimmed
bloodshot eyes
behind her
all-too-familiar
cacophonous shuffle
past
ashen-faced

amorphous entity
cackles and taunts
ubiquitous
merciless.

She walks
always forward
gradually widening
strips of sunlight

holding onto hope

Sally resides in Birmingham, Alabama.

Pain is the pen that purges my past and carves a path towards
the promise of a tomorrow. Allpoetry.com/smc

[Stephen Hollins]

a snowflake

I drive from silver steel skylines
and glass towers
returning to dig my hot feet
in horizon's cool red earth
to breathe within the naked wood

leaving behind the businesspeople
and employees who wrestle daily
in brain blocked organizations
fighting and struggling to
emerge into networks of co-creation

whereas the earth mother
organizes herself
without organizing

take a simple snowflake for example
water vapor condenses onto a
falling nascent starlight ice crystal

tiny hexagonal branching plates sprout
arms spiraling through fluffy clouds
icy astronaut ballerinas duetting
with temperature and humidity

the crystalline body of earth mother's
breath a sparkling diamond snowflake

created by the precise path it dances
sprouting in sculptural synchrony
balconied ice labyrinths of structure

no two snow crystals fly the same path
and no two mirrors the same shape

the world's landlady asks for no rent
daily whispering life's music in the ears
of her tenants, that hear her not

her great engine fires few pistons
that do not wear out
waters brewing, golden fields and flowers blossom
no rest in rusting, yet peace is her sleep

she takes no counsel with historians
museums, shareholders or churches
lives life now, in the company of the universe

her planet constantly rotates
as she renews her audience

mother earth cloaks man
in a veil of darkness
leaving him digging
for the gold
in light

I am loving writing poetry. I live on Waiheke Island. New Zealand. I specialize in Improv for Theatre, Acting, Storytelling, Dance, Clown, Mime, Teaching, Building. Allpoetry.com/Stephen_Hollins

[Lisa F. Raines]
And I'm not gonna make it home

Why do I want to go home,
when you're not there anymore?

Why do I say goodbye every day,
when I wish you were here?

Why do I cry, try, dry my eyes,
deny my cries, decry my life?

Fight, flight, slight light, always right;
Lie, lie, lie, lie, lie, lie, LIE

———————————

AlisRamie is from North Carolina, USA.
Interests include: philosophy, history, international relations,
poetry, art, design, jazz, funk, and some good old soul.
Allpoetry.com/AlisRamie

[Lisa F. Raines]

Life Lost

Let
Liars
Lie
Lovers'
Love
Lost

A six word story. AlisRamie is from North Carolina, USA.
Interests include: philosophy, history, international relations,
poetry, art, design, jazz, funk, and some good old soul.
Allpoetry.com/AlisRamie

[David I Mayerhoff]
Peeling the Layers

A floor creaks
while the overhead squeaks-
a missing screw
fallen into the sea of shoes below

The door beckons enter
on the strata of life
revealing forgotten footprints
in a terrain of trials
and joys

An insect buzzes
by the distant socks
as it seeks a match
for a blue argyle
sitting solitary in the corner

An old shirt
long outgrown by girth and style
shining a spotlight
on more athletic days

A blood stained handkerchief
escaping the eye of the cleaner
after a large nosebleed

Boots knee high

walking on rough terrain
a suit once worn
with cap and gown
announcing I am
meeting the world
on its terms

Nestled in the back
a sweater with bright patterns
given as a gift
speaking of a special encounter
and lasting bonds
in a closet
with a life's memories turned
inside out

_____

David I Mayerhoff is an emerging literary writer, an
established scientific author and a Clinical Professor of
Psychiatry. Allpoetry.com/David_Mayerhoff

[Evan Palmer]

Hark! The Golden Ampersand!

A gift left on a doorstep
waiting to be opened
by a golden pharaoh.

On the tip of a porcelain tongue
sits a lonely soliloquy
preparing to slide off at the wrong moment.

Collections of closets melting into hallways
melting into bedrooms melting into one large house that
contains
a case of ivory tusks seated in a black marble chair.

Evan is from Michigan and is currently attending Kalamazoo
College. He writes in his free time and some common themes
in his poems are the moon and gardens.
Allpoetry.com/quasarous

[Amber Alana Hodge]

In Time

Your love is finer than wine
Brought forth from a very good year
aged to perfection in time
turn your ear to the hourglass of my rhyme
the grain is falling
my words are calling
silver and brown
are such lovely colors
atop a lovely crown
silver in your left hand
and gold upon your head
listen close, my love
as you lie in bed
the night is falling
and the master of the house is calling

_____

I love to write. I am 33 years old from Greenville TX. I love to write biblically inspired work as well as love poetry. Allpoetry.com/Amber_A._Hodge

[Sofia Hällgren]

Nirvanarain

She looks like an actress.
She rides the slide in nirvanarain.
She is a head   Then she isn't.
Awakened.
Satani. Raingods,
Rainroom. She isn't here.
Raingirls parkas. Yellow
Made by ladies seamstresses
In fantasyland.. magilia.
Those were witches...
And dream is the fabric.
Sewing night and day.
She's interested in
Art on a leaf.
She is made by rainbows. Rainbows drawn by a
Girl in a rainbow room.
Where dead people draw and write.
Art. Opened it and ... the
Sun marries Al Capone's husband.

I'm 39 years of age and I am a student, archeology, at
University in Umeå. I am interested in Writing, the arts,
poetry, watching nature, Movies, animals, will hopefully
study law. (If I get in) Allpoetry.com/Sofia_Hellgren

[Jonathan Moya]

The Love Stories and Tragedies of Trash

Swept up in the last row of the balcony of an old movie palace
with crushed red velvet chairs:
• one crumbled ticket for Gone in 60 Seconds,
• a golden tub with unspoken kernels
and a hole big enough for the popcorn trick,
• three invisible blonde hairs from a future wife.

Thrown away from the backseat of a screaming yellow taxi:
• the left corner piece of an hand printed
Our House poster held at a Antonio Delgado
swearing in rally,
• a cocktail napkin with vibrant lipstick smears
from Snapper Magee's,
• the hardened remains of a McFlurry with nuts
dribbled from fingers kissed.

Tossed in with the other drawstring containers in a green
curbside bin in front of the family house for Eileen:
• the price tag for a Blue Nile Studio
Petite French Pavé Crown
Diamond Engagement Ring
in Platinum and another for
• a Cowboy wedding band,
• seven revised proposals
written on a yellow legal pad,
• two more on what to say to her father.

Discarded in the same bin nine months later:
• the unwoven knitting of an Afghanistan war widow—
scarves, gloves, a camouflage hat with pom-poms.

Found in the dumpster of the Royal Pavilion Wedding Hall
after the nuptials of Frank and Jane:
• a wedding program printed
on aged-look parchment,
• the crumbles of a three tier wedding cake-
the first layer tiramisu,
the second white chocolate mousse,
the third a carrot cake without walnuts
for the food allergen prone,
• monogrammed napkins with
FM/JO printed in baby's breaths blue
in the right hand corner,
• the broken heel of
an imitation Manolo Blahnik,
• the wilting petals of red roses and dahlias.

Found covered up in baby shower wrapping paper left at the
curb of Jane and Frank's House:
• a paint sample card
with five shades of little blue,
• a lab report with a positive diagnosis,
• a broken rattle,
• a pacifier with a torn nipple,
• a dirty diaper,
• a mother's tears in a folded napkin,
• a father's regretful words
buried deep on a thumbnail drive.

Among the detritus of their house with a FOR SALE sign:
• The unneeded gem paper clip
after the dissolution papers
had been stapled and signed,
• five forgive me reminders
written on 3x5 index cards,
• a yellow post-it note with NEVER!
written on top of them,
• all their photo albums
enshrouded in vellum binders.

Noticed in the elevated trash bins at the cemetery where Jane
is to be buried:
• the printed out e-mail excuses
for those who heard but
were too busy to come,
• the dirt off the hands
of those who did,
• the soiled paper plates of
those who ate at the wake.

The things left behind at Frank's potter's funeral:
• no one,
• nothing,
• not a thing.

I am a retired shopkeeper and former Walt Disney World cast
member who lives to write about movies and some poetry.
Allpoetry.com/Jonathan_Moya

[Kyle Garon]

A Nightmare and a Wolf

I have the dream again,
January blaze
eyes laying glaze
to a sleeping midnight air,
except I wasn't alone.
Mounted or rather laced
by murmuring trees
bound to a tatter stained
wolf,
watching soullessly breathe
it's maw dripping; like rain drops on steel.
Blinded by its shade
hazy lavender girl,
wearing a pale dress
blending over her flesh.
She cries within my site,
the hirsute demon
devouring her, I'm helpless
watching the winter fields be drenched.
I'm awaken to the howling dawn,
her voice soothes me
and my nightmares are erased.

———————————

Poetry has been a constant in the last Nine years. I wouldn't
know what else I would do. Poet for life.
Allpoetry.com/Lucius_Moon

[Kim Van Breda]

Occluded

senseless, this mind
filled with ghosts that
came and went, bent
priceless on panic
in debt I pace
to silence embraced

slipping away
off ancient charts,
occluded

jungle creatures
eight legged black
predators that snack
I turn, trench coat
white dappled backed
parasol attack

chipping away
at wooden hearts,
occluded

———————————

I bend toward the abstract side of poetry and enjoy poets with depth who pull you into their writes with a touch of intrigue. Poetry and swimming feed my soul. Allpoetry.com/Mermaid

[Kathryn Kass]

Black Beauty

grief a diet pill
curbs appetite for living
crows fatten on nuts

thump, thump, thump, thump, thump
hot blood seeks volcanic vent
a breaking heart blows

loss on the menu
I can barely swallow air
salty taste of tears

Kathryn lives near the ocean in southern California. She feeds the crows that call at her kitchen door. Hummingbirds inspire her to seek nectar and find the poetry in every experience. Allpoetry.com/Katekass7

[Margaret M Murray]

Material Girl

I couldn't find a fried egg print
or a giant slice of emmental
on brilliant red designed to shock
I see black cabs driving through rain
and a silk fringe that could shimmy
on the hem of my charleston frock

Elegant as a catwalk queen
as poised as her left-handed shears
she cuts through my blue crepe de chine

Her right hand is closed in a fist
like a tight bud waiting for spring
or flower power, the green therapist

We talk of sewing, upcycling and
how to save the planet, but I
have no amulet to heal her hand

She has her own talisman, sheer
bravura and a strong left arm.
I think *bravo* and silently cheer

_____

I love reciting poems and occasionally write one, normally
when something or someone inspires me.   I also like painting
portraits of my family, drama and jazz dancing
Allpoetry.com/Margetmurray98

121

[Alwyn Barddylbach]

There's a Blackbird in my Garden

I can lead and I can charm
the old world rhymer that
kept me company while
tending in my garden;

Song of a wild blackbird
sweeter than a cherry.

Once with princely
psalm and breed this
little gendarme had so
many tales to sing about.

We'd turn the soil,
dig up weed and bless
the sun together disarmed
in mindful conversation.

Lost for worms he'd come
looking for me, hopping
on my sunny windowsill,
raven preen and cunning;

Pockets full of rye
chanting on counterpoint.

Haunted crackles of

dissent crow on the fence,
claim jealous and cocky,
gabble and greed.

Come ready this trap
and caution bleed,
chop off your heads for
tomorrow is a dainty dish.

But steady and bright
in court concede,
plumbaginous canticles
succoured in flight;

Fly four and twenty
up into the sky.

I miss the company
and who will miss a feed?
Think not of pie nor nosey
high and mighty heed;

It's not the disingenuous
who die.

Remembering rhymes of yesterday, our pockets full of rye,
your money or your song - Aussie Quatrain AB, Blue
Mountains. Allpoetry.com/Barddylbach

[Tony Noon]
Untouched Envelopes

My hands are probably famous now.
Some novel, a poem maybe,
describing the texture.
The span of my ringed fingers.

I saw the sideways glance.
Quick notes beside
thumbnails of Lowry porters
and the dull paraphernalia
of suburban platforms.

My hands may have an alias now.
Skills ascribed to them
in some thick plot.

Pushing envelopes I never touched.

Tony Noon lives in Mexborough , South Yorkshire. His
poems have been widely anthologised as well as appearing in
local and national newspapers and magazines.
Allpoetry.com/TonyNoon642

[Deepak Haridas]
The Proteas tumbleweed

Point blank bullets
soaked in crimson red
Triggered by perspective
myopia, it can't see
Soweto and Sharpeville,
drenched in blood
conjuring visions unbowed
while the soil bleeds.

Rolling downhill ,
a whimsical tumbleweed
knitted together through despair,
pain and anguish
Wobbling and skimming
against cultural greed
Bumping on signs
of " blanke gebied"
Puffing dust
(of Apartheid)
as the winds recede.

Originally from India , Deepak lives in Berlin . An IT entrepreneur by profession , he takes passion in writing stories and poetry during free time hopes to positively inspire the readers . Allpoetry.com/Pandaboy

[Amber Alana Hodge]

A Happy Ending

Snow covered mountains
a cabin atop a hill
a fireplace burning with cedar
red wine to our fill
the joy of the Lord fueling the flame
our hearts beating together the same
the days of like no end and no beginning
wool and flax on a wheel that is spinning
the sound of children laughing and playing
in the house we are staying
where time has no end
people with hearts on the mend
the days of sickness and death long past
our Savior has come at last

———————————

I love to write. I am 33 years old from Greenville TX. I love
to write biblically inspired work as well as love poetry.
Allpoetry.com/Amber_A._Hodge

[Isaac Munoz]

Marathon Runner

You can tread along pavement,
dirt or rock,
dragging on with worn-out shoes,
and miraculously,
be not defined by the blood you bleed
from calloused feet,
but by the miles under you.
26.2.

From L.A., struggled with weight all my life, after losing 80
pounds, I went back to run the L.A. marathon. This poem is a
reminder that it's not where I've been that defines me, but
where im going. Allpoetry.com/Pompadour_Poet

[Jemma M]

The Choice

I am a ray of sunshine on a warm summer's day
I am the sound of laughter of children at play
I am the starlight that shines on lovers at night
I am a young family cuddled up warm and tight

My voice sings a song from the gods above
My heart emanates intimate and infinite pure love

I am an ocean that sparkles like diamonds dancing on blue silk
I am a newborn held lovingly, nurtured by her mother's milk
I am the fertile wilderness in perfect harmony with all living
things
I am creativity and expression delivered by divinity's wings

My eyes observe and I want to surrender
My mind is hopeful all this I will remember

For I am also the darkness and pain in a country without
beauty
I am the tears of young orphan's sudden adult duties
I am the smoke that rises from industrial pollution
I am contaminated water and famine without solution

My voice without sound, the gods above seem apathetic
My heart wants to reach out, but soon enough I will forget it

I am an ocean littered in toxic waste now poisoning its own

I am a mother's stillborn, a dream, never meant to grow
I am drought, devastation, disease, and death
I am the abandoned aged as she draws her last breath

My eyes are tearful from the sights that I see
My mind is desperate to deny the misery

I am an angel and I am a demon
I build and destroy without logic or reason
I am passion, love, anger and hate
I can imprison and I can emancipate

I am human and I am the universe
I am god too; this is my curse
Overwhelming responsibility and unnerving control
I realize the potential and power of this role

Existence so random and without instruction,
The choice for growth or for destruction.

Jemma M is from Vancouver, BC. Poetry has been the best
therapy in my experience. I'm always open to the journey of
learning, guidance, and self-improvement.
Allpoetry.com/Jemma_M

[Arlice W Davenport]

What the Blind Man Heard

Halfway up the stairs to the bone-white, beehive Basilica of
Sacre-Coeur, I lost count of my climb. My legs remembered
every trembling step, but they could no longer do the math -
On the vast portico, swarming with earnest worker bees,
guidebooks in hand, I turned to take in the triumphant,
panoramic view of smog-shrouded Paris -- a vision marred by
the massive carbon boot print of 11 million Parisians.

As my stomach snarled from my meager morning meal, I
searched for a place to eat my equally meager lunch. Soon, I
spied a bench wide enough for three people, but with only one
occupant, an old Frenchman, blind from childhood. As I
watched the tourist crowds run amok, careering into one
another, I asked if I could sit down beside him, and we struck
up a conversation in French.

Affable, intelligent, alert as a bird among cats, he was reading
a braille biography of Marie Antoinette. I was impressed. He
then told me how as a result of an untreatable eye disease, he
had had his optic nerves cut as a boy. It was a drastic measure,
to be sure, but common at the time.

Now, he said, his life nearly over, he seriously contemplated
suicide, plagued by the meaningless daily routine of a visit to
Sacre- Coeur, where he rested, a fixture unseen by the
unsettling crowds. He could find no other purpose.

So, thinking myself a therapist to the world, I leaned in close and remarked, "There is always hope." "Why do you say this?" "Because God exists." "Ah, God exists," he retorted in a half-question, half-scoff.

Below, the carousel's calliope played a delightful, dancing tune. He listened intently. After that, we sat silently side by side for several minutes, he hearing the shuffling feet, I watching the mobs of visitors overrun the balcony. We never spoke again, until it was time for me to enter the basilica. We exchanged "adieux," and I walked away. To this day, I wonder what the blind man heard, among the noisome crowds, on his lonely bench at the base of the beehive Sacre-Coeur.

Paris is one of the greatest cities in the world, but also one of the most difficult to develop relationships with strangers. This poem documents an extreme counter example. The serendipity amazes me. Allpoetry.com/arliced

[Sandra Joann Ray]

Nico

Some think I came too early
But I was part of His plan
From my Creator who formed me
With the palm of his hand

He knew me by name
Before I was placed in the womb
You may not have known I'd come so soon
But I came in his perfect time, I assume

I saw the fear in Mommy & Daddy's eyes
As I came to them that day
Everyone came together to pray
To plead with heaven that I would be okay

Mommy & Daddy wished
I would've remained inside her
But God needed me here on earth right now
To be his little reminder

I came to this earth
In such a fragile state
They all were so worried
Because I was so underweight

Mommy & Daddy, I know it hasn't been easy
I still have struggles to this day

But remember God has been faithful
And has surely made a way

So I'm here to remind you
Of the greatness of God
And how strong a tiny thing can be
When the hand of the Lord rest upon it mightily

Mommy & Daddy
You may face a mountain
You may face a storm
You may face a giant
And be tattered and torn

But always know that no matter
How far you go
God will find you
Remember Mommy & Daddy
My life is here to remind you!

———————————

Sandra Joann Ray is from Fremont, Ohio. Poetry helps me express myself and cope with the storms of my life. I use my poetry to testify of the unconditional love, amazing grace and goodness of God! Allpoetry.com/Sandrasmilesagain1

[Sofia Hällgren]

I art

We are, we aren't.

Artbooks morguewater.

She sews a waterdress for a doll.

With raindrops from autumn Japan.

An artdeal broker, while she plays witch.

With faeries. A scream of the butterfly.

It is art, a seastars exhibition, cloudbooks. I watch a concert in the sky.

Cloud dolls. I. Dodo weeps.

From japan, she comes. A sewing lady

Sewing a whole dreamdoll with threads from a spiderweb from Guatemala.

A nightmare dreamweaver....

A unicorn. Funeralhouse.

Edith Whartons poetry ,

My art. Extinct animals

At the zoo.

Im smoking with the rastaboys...

I'm 39 years of age and I am a student, archeology, at University in Umeå.

I am interested in Writing, the arts, poetry, watching nature, Movies, animals, will hopefully study law. (If I get in)
Allpoetry.com/Sofia_Hellgren

134

[Edward a Torres]
Like a painting

her curves
elegantly flow
with the breeze blowing the blades of grass
or the ripples in the bluest of rivers
her pink lips
softer than the red petals swaying around us
her honey brown eyes sparkle and lighten
when the summer sun meets.

she is like a painting
smiling
her ivory skin perfectly contrasts
the lavender and blue bonnet filled meadow,
as the wild perfumed Texas wind,
sways her raven black hair,
the perfect muse for a brush or quill

_____

I am from San Antonio, Texas. I love to write about personal experiences and memories. My goal is to be published and hopefully my writing makes people feel understood.
Allpoetry.com/Edward_Torres

[Alec Dnine]

Father's smile

Fine gravels crepitate under my feet:
low-high, low-high, low-high,
I stroll through quiet pathways in the park.
Every few moments air moves so faintly
But I notice, for it is refreshing.

The trunks of old sequoias probably take five adults
To try embracing, though maybe four for cedars.
So I conjecture that they must have seen
Ten? Or fifteen? Or more, of trying generations.

That waft was stronger!
Coming from the right,
It broke the piny lull,
It made heart cramp
And double up the pace,
The eyes got tingly,
All this in a trice.
I couldn't recognize
At first the scent
Slight, sweet and sharp.
I turned behind
The yew shrub.

A flowerbed lay there, full of sumptuous blossoms
Resembling peonies, but bright: red, orange, yellow.
I haven't seen such tulips, and they were,

Exuding an aroma of the ones my father used to plant,
But in another garden, by another lake... I stood there long.

Lived and worked in different countries, now in Switzerland.
Came back to writing and translating poetry recently, after a
gap of many years. Photography, travels, running also give
me energy. Allpoetry.com/Alec_Dnine

[Sofia Hällgren]

The night lasted long enough

She rose out of bed, a towel draped over her. She leaned towards the statue of Virgin Mary statue that was next to a unicorn and garlands of fairy light.

She put a sea star in her hair as she left, she put her makeup kit besides the tomato plant. She left, her room still scenting as teenage soul perfume as she did. She said hello to the gardener and the neighbours as they waved. She waved and left, a faint silhouette against the summer street. Her friends already had bathing suits on as she was going to swim, July was here as she loved to swim. She left singing for the changing room. The sky was hazel and azure the sea. They saw the kids, and parents and couples bathing, their beach tents put up. Sky had slit its wrists to bleed across the sky and sun was setting. Fairylike, she sat there, Lucy, with her long golden brown hair. Tattooed with an angel to cover up scars. She sat bolt upright and put on sunscreen as she was eyed by all males.

She lay down as nautical wind blew across her face and she jumped into the sea swimming. No one knew about their plans. Stars appeared as they later lay on their backs, talking about God. They drank alcohol-free beer as they smoked cloves. Incense smell and beer as the smoke rose like souls toward the sky...
We're going to meet him soon....she smiled. All the girls took a sip of soda as they reached up their fingers v signs. The

glitter and their crosses glittered in the moonlight...the beach lay silent...deserted. They resembled Deaths pale daughters already. So far, the schools most loveliest perfect goddess like creatures.

I'm 39 years of age and I am a student, archeology, at University in Umeå.

I am interested in Writing, the arts, poetry, watching nature, Movies, animals, will hopefully study law. (If I get in)
Allpoetry.com/Sofia_Hellgren

[Jessyka Mcallister]

Beast

Withered fingers clenched the Earth
Bringing forth the storm within
Slowly pouring the grounds of the past
Releasing the caged beast
Teethed bared ready to strike
To take control, to be free
Foreign powers radiate through my veins,
a poison taking its course
Flashes of light breaks through the caliginous sky
roaring skies above
Give me the strength to carry on,
to cage the beast once again

Jessyka McAllsiter currently lives in Bristol VA. I am a mom of 5 wonderful and beautiful children. I write to escape from daily world of chaos. Allpoetry.com/JessyMac

[Duncan Wagner]

Rachel

Tied to these words
I untie you, set you to

what's over, last rites
finally breathing, shape rising from an empty room

Of all the beauties, You remain unknown
last corridor into blue

under the bolted lights
airless, unchristened, unformed

An anonymous figure
menaces from the edge

From years past
what was said, what's remembered

what's lost

I live between New England and Florida. I have been involved with Allpoetry since 2007 or whereabouts. I have been writing poetry since 1990. Allpoetry.com/Duncan_Wagner

[Sharon Mooney]

Swimming the Tide

The bahia had personality today
I swam in humid afternoon
alone just bobbing up and down, lazy.
The sea on the other hand
was what workshop leaders call assertive,
waves of afternoon's incoming tide
laid full up against my upright body
pushing me softly and swiftly
along the edge of my dock.

Usually I can dreamily stroke through the water
and keep face to face with the ladder
but today he was in the mood to claim me.
Not just move me out of the way
like the wakes of passing boats
but like someone bigger who
knows his power and uses it
to take me with him or
make me press to get back my berth.

Not a wiggler or swimmer beneath his surface
clear for at least twelve feet down into mysterious dark.
The bahia was alive with being
rolling, pushing forward into nowhere
alive with lustiness to overpower me
like a trusted lover's insistent seducing.
I turned my face down to his wet countenance

and smiled into his potent swell
moving me out of my safe spot
trying to pull me into his indigo currents.

———————————

Bahia is Spanish for bay. I have been writing for more than
35 years. It is a life stream of mine. I live on the Sea of Cortez
in northern Mexico. Aging, death & the spirit of life are
repeating topics in my prose and poetry.
Allpoetry.com/WriteMexico

[Rebecca Hopwood]

Miss Becky & Mr. Jim, 1959

stormy October night
porcelain white girl, age of 10
name, Miss Becky
wild winds whipping round
bright lights striking a moody sky
with all encompassing thunder that
sounded like forever
to her

same stormy night
a handyman, black as midnight with no moon
name, Mr. Jim
peeking through tiny windows at the top
of the front door to Miss Becky's house
drenching rain pelting sideways
felt like a worrisome situation
to him

banging on the door, interrupting the downpour
Mr. Jim booms the ask
"Are you and your Mama alright?"
Miss Becky and Mama hurried the door
led Mr. Jim to the warm open fire
snacked on freshly popped corn
drank Mama's homemade fizzy beverage
together

thirty years came and passed
Miss Becky and Mr. Jim visited often
as good friends do
Together they authored a mutual eulogy-
If the only ask is 'Are you alright?'
never mind if you're black or white.

———————————————

A world without poetry would implode. I do my best to
contribute positively and as expertly as I can. Every day is a
gift to learn, express, connect. Allpoetry.com/Skysummer54

[Manvi Goel]

A glimpse of azure on an icy island

Draped with a parched semblance,
roped in a succumbed existence,
enswathed by the deceit of crafty illusions,
tarnished with the havoc of vivacious visions,
the veins of skeleton,
lied benumbed on the arctic ocean,
gazing towards the path unknown,
that too was inert and standing alone.
As the two stones ingrained with agony,
caught the sight of each others melancholy,
the rhythms of enigma echoed,
survival and uncertainties,
success and difficulties,
are like archery board and dart,
they cannot be drifted apart,
canvassing the butter-milked sky,
from glacial to an incarnadine sight,
is an art,
an art of carving out an emerald from barren,
crystallized with the ashes of ashen.
Dyeing the breadth of view with the iridescence of dyed
vision,
sculpting an anemic vista from grayish to crimson,
while connecting the dots with the chords of aesthetic sense,
and beholding the blessings in present tense,
enlivens up the artistry of

creating optimistic vibes,
and dancing to the tunes of melodious chimes.

I am from India . I am a nature lover .I love being artistic and
exploring the unexplored things in this world. I believe in
living alive every moment of life. Love your life, life will
love you back. Allpoetry.com/Manvi_Goel

[Jacob Robert Gallo Ofiana]
destroying protection

the trenches we dug outside
has collected the water
and now small animals
use our barrier as a pool
we thickened the trees
to protect our skin from the sun
now the birds use it to nest in
we had the machine guns as weapons
but now they are only designs
this house was used for the protection
yet it became a magnet of life
the tear between the world
only was used to let things in
we painted all of the scratches on the door
we took the roof and walls down
we didn't want the restrictions of home
we had the world to live in
one place can't be our home forever
for we can live all over
the nature we stayed away from
developed all around us
that it cracked through the window
broke all of my past ideas
I want to go outside
and keep breaking down these walls

Jacob Gallo from Gilroy California. I write these poems the difference between beauty and lies. That just because we are safe doesn't mean that we are living.
Allpoetry.com/Mark_Toleway

[Sonja Carnes]

Sleepless Night

Lush green valley greets the moon
Appearing in the west, I witness a lunar shimmering crest
Fully ripe in glow, sister stars dance to and fro
Moonbeams lace the valley as night begins to grow
Cradled between the mountain supreme majesty softly shows
Shadows of the dark turn my eyes to midnights might
A captivating sight
When the glory of this moment start to light,
This valley walks the sleepless night

My Father was born in Sicily, later his Father and Mother
Came to America. I am first generation of my Fathers line.
My Mother is French and was a really good song writer.
Thank You. Allpoetry.com/Allseasonsverse

[Celine Cheung]

Satsuma

Spiced peels, citrus unshiu
the orange sanctuary of serenity;
of scented scrubs washing exhaustion,
or awakened scents igniting minds
one silken touch, I'm in sensual heaven

Or perhaps, one soothing sniff -
I am in perfumed exotica
of Japanese meticulousness and Spanish suns
a lotion drop, or a seedless bite
softly invoking unspoken gentleness

awaken me with sunshine

Celine Cheung is a writer based in Toronto and Hong Kong
who loves all things coffee, inter-cultural and beautiful.
Allpoetry.com/gothchyld

[Alison B. Emery]

the art of mental illness

mental illness
is an art form
she conjures careful
delusions through
abstract realities
such as the rapture
Is coming now,
and seeing
Angels in
parking lots.
with a cocked head,
and shaking hands -
the bewildered
brush strokes begins

painting the eyes
of a mad painter-
disillusioned dreams
splash
white canvas
ever so gently
upon an unsteady easel
a permanent picture
dries -
and hence a palette of
mismatched colors
of blues & blacks

to confuse the patrons
at her gala

Alison B. Emery is a Wife, Bunny Mom, Nurse, Co-Owner of
Shoestring Book Publishing, Board Member of the
International Poetry Fellowship, Poetry & Story Blogger, and
a published Author Allpoetry.com/DeviantPixie

[Z Valkyrie]

Abandoned

He squealed on the floor
seeing angels and demons,
broken and bloody,
held down for his sake
and for those he attacked,
in a delirium he thrashed

A flood surged to break
from the dam of my eyes
crested as looking skyward
shooting stars soared above,
streaking sparks through the pins
of light flickering dust.

A beacon of relief, still he wriggled
as the stars soothed the waves.

I'm no scholar but writing provides clarity, focus, freedom. It
brings back something long lost, heals an ache that seemed
incurable and delivers stability in the shakiest hours - a source
of strength Allpoetry.com/ZValkyrie

[Patricia Marie Batteate]

Animals are People Too

A visit to the zoo
A milestone for any child
Every animal imaginable
Most of them wild

The best view by far
Was from the neck of a giraffe
The hyenas were always good
For a hideous laugh

The bears all sprawled out
Basking in the sun
The elephants easily weighed
A couple of tons

The motionless alligators
Laid silently in wait
One step over the edge
You've signed your own fate

The zebras all dressed
In zen black and white
The seagulls above
Soared in flight

The hippos kept cool
Submerged in water

The occasional splash
Of the playful sea otter

The apes, so human
One had to think
Are we related
By the missing link

The lions all napping
In between meals
The crowd entertained
By the California seals

The monkeys all swinging
From limb to limb
Their antics derived
Solely by whim

The snakes all coiled
And neatly wound
The bird's contributing
To most of the sound

The animals by far
Where not amused
In fact they looked bored
And a bit confused

They miss their birth place
They once had known

Even they can't deny
There's no place like home.

I am a 7th generation Californian. I am an engineer, poet and
artist. I could see poets inheriting the earth.

Allpoetry.com/Patricia_Marie

[Alwyn Barddylbach]

One Verse at a Time:

Beyond Nineveh's Plains

One is the opening whim to greet my day,
announcement on the morning radio,
the weather report. Tea drinkers around the
world like me ordering coffee.

Two is where I'd drink that coffee
on the edge of my seat none too proud.

Three is that sensation
on the back of my neck
as I take in the morning sun,
lost for words.

Four is that sinking thought in the bottom
of my cup, the employer who makes us
anxious, could have been a tragic case
but who's to know unhappy?

Five is a shroud, how long it takes to leave
a job without a shred of guilt or doubt,
time I ditched the defence mechanism.

Six is what we sacrifice at work,
my only regret
the real life we've all been missing.

So seven I sigh
sanctuary, idle,
peace at last having
read the poem

.

Beyond Nineveh's Plains

Good morning sleepers,
oven roasted buns and
chestnut brown espresso in
the air. It's freshly toasted
tropical sunrise over Java
and savour those skies.
Ozone blue all day
dripping on thunder,
maple syrup and powdery
pancakes late afternoon.

Clouds dissolve
in waterfall canyon
to marmalade breakfast
and stunning sounds of
white cockatoo below,
gliding on thermals like tiny
marshmallows inscribed
on the insides of your coffee cup.

These sandstone cliffs
drop away skydiving

into the bottom of my belly,
pushing and lifting me up
into empty sky. Sun gazing
endlessly at the half eaten
cake of an old moon landing,
halfway light headed.
I am breathing in the bark
of red gum on the edge
of Three Sister's rock,
crowned in the sun's corona.

My cup is empty at ten o'clock.
I look up at the solitary mountain
as my smart phone's dulcet tones
remind me of the remainder
of the day. Stomach churns
like an inland sea as the
mid-morning monster swallows
me whole in its gaping jaws.

Jonah, Jonah I scream,
hiding in the bowels of
Nineveh's plains, guts
hanging out tearing at
the cosmos of my sandbag
world, the gods want your blood!
The thunderstorm came earlier
than the radio predicted,
swirling like the great river of Oz.
I'm safe as houses in my tin can,
arms uncovered, washed in

the deluge of tropical rain.

One verse at a time
the great elder happily tells me,
standing at the foot of
the Giant Stairway,
pointing his trembling finger
at top of Dardanelles Pass.
The black cockatoo is
struck by white lightning,
the sky cracked open
ozone blue. Many great
grandchildren fall out of
the cloud, the sisters cried.

Tap tap feint crackle,
the radio died. Tools lie idle
and waters weeping plunge
down the mountainside.

Without the transformative beauty of nature's idylls around us
we'd never be free to recognise the prisons we created and
worked in, except briefly in our coffee break - AB, Blue
Mountains, Australia. Allpoetry.com/Barddylbach

[Stephen Hollins]

after drinking the black milk

I found her face in a brown paper bag
at the back of an oak closet
she looks unsmiling down and left
this young exotic girl, a movie star? or fashion model?
half Chinese half French, where east meets west
dressed in an ornamental gold silk collared robe
head stands on strong broad shoulders

hands folded inside a pale brown hessian tunic
painted in a restricted but vibrant palette of vivid intensity
luxuriant full-bodied black hair frames
her face a distinctive turquoise blue and green
skin tones of copper shades brushed onto cheekbones

plump closed lips painted with
glossy red max-factor lipstick
her pregnant and subdued expression
casts a hypnotic trance catches the eye

Chinese Girl is Tretchikoff's best-known work
printed as a hugely popular poster
in millions of homes all around the world
the highest selling art print in history

a worldwide phenomenon and postwar classic
not only to Europeans and the Commonwealth
but also to Orientals and Africans

parading in a labyrinth of living room walls
the green lady is found on mugs, cushions
wallpaper, t-shirts, and collectibles

is she the eastern queen seductress?
dragon lady or the oriental pageant jewel?
frowned on by Nazi art watchdogs
an extraordinary young lady
courted by millions of ordinary people

who wanted to travel to foreign lands
to raise their hopes and aspirations
after drinking the black milk of two world wars
men and women the color of lead
posting dreams into clouds

I am loving writing poetry I live on Waiheke Island New
Zealand. I specialize in Improv for Theatre, Acting,
Storytelling, Dance, Clown, Mime, Teaching, Building.
Allpoetry.com/Stephen_Hollins

[Duncan Wagner]

Menage

I watch the dark trace
of what's left of you

as it recedes
and this time

I'm half-free
while your white torso, an emulsion

alabaster, perfect and pear-like
reclining amongst the confines of that room

Your head turned, while the moon
hid amongst your paleness, as if to say, "no more"

You, most equal to a City before daylight
Stirrings, new manhood, an April night

Yet we were never lovers,

So afraid I was of those dark eyes,
anthracite, while you devoured me

The line of your lips, thin and pursed
trying to say something, fed into night

reaching to a place, where I was not allowed to stay

You, an idea, my being, a path without footprints

a basket of stones

Still morning
Paula wakening

You stepped frozen
to the other side

The bridge, how
it has all but disappeared

Lighting a cigarette
at the moment where I lost you

like a man finding
for the first time

the meaning of his loneliness
or the secrets of his name.

I am from Boston Mass. I currently live in rural New England.
I have been writing poetry since 1990. I have been involved
with Allpoetry since about 2007.
Allpoetry.com/Duncan_Wagner

[David Burrows]

On the Paintings of Clyfford Still

You look at his ebony
blotches of paint
and Momma kisses you,
places you
in a bassinet.

He pours red, orange, blue
all hues
to make black
abstract
shapes,
to mix his embrace.

As if you say
"I'll take one with everything,"
and he dips his brush
into the rainbow,
caresses across
the creamy canvas
of your skin,
invites you
into the dark
holy

David has resided in Denver, CO for twenty years. Poetry makes his heart and brain happy. David has written several children's musicals, hymns and choral anthems. Allpoetry.com/Heartflute

[Marilyn Griffin]

Dear All Poetry

teach me the flight of words
the weight and depth and
height of them

but not on a sunny day-

phrases festooned with
nouns ballooned-
no

teach me the richness of
memory-world
shrunk to one thought
like an african daisy in
acres of cracked cement

teach me an apt place to scream
or calm
teach me to wait in
an empty field
arms open to
the hard and lost

teach me soft

This is a true letter to Allpoetry and Kevin, whom I owe a huge thanks to! I love this site, thanks to all the wonderful friends I've made. You all all my teachers!
Allpoetry.com/Greeningofautumn

[Manvi Goel]

Twilight of a chromatic amour

With the dawn of an hour of twilight,
under the haven of a chromatic skylight,
the swain of cosmos,
wings his way through the ether
with the ecstasy of a bird like flutter,
yodeling with a rosy tinged smile
that is eternal and vivacious,
he bows down on the horizon
in the awe of enchantress of tranquility,
who is adorable and gracious.
The heaven kindles a beacon of love,
to embrace the lady love,
draped in a dove like semblance,
glammed up with a tinge of a seraphic fragrance,
ready for a walk on the crest,
flowering a gust of breeze imbued with zest,
and unfurls a rug,
tinted with the shade of blue tulips,
honoring the euphoric cupids.
Whilst the moment of this sacred rendezvous springs in with a
musk,
the romeo of the dusk,
glows in the trance of a divine amour,
and goes reddish orange with ardour,
the panorama twinkles with a rainbow like hue,
and bestows the islands of the blessed with a heart stirring
view.

Adorned with a garland of an incandescent flambeau,
in the lap of a cherubic ambience,
as immaculate as a morning dew,
the moment crystal like lagoon,
mirrors this awe – inspiring view,
the waves of freedom ripples,
the tides of joy giggles,
and liveliness unfurls.

I am from India .I am a nature lover .I love being artistic and exploring the unexplored things in this world. I believe in living alive every moment of life.Love your life life will love you back

Allpoetry.com/Manvi_Goel

[Joseph Giso]

Old Man

"No good deed goes unpunished, "
said the old man as he laid down for his final rest.

kindness rewarded with malice.

he understood and welcomed peace into his heart,
shuttered his eyes and warmed his face with a smile.

Joe Giso is CPA who is also fond of words and their meaning.
Accountant with a passion for words all their meanings. From
Italy and now settled in Massachusetts with a wife and two
adult children. Allpoetry.com/Jgisocpa

[Patricia M Wynn]
High School Blues

a freshman child so shy and coy
admiringly stares at the sophomore boy
the sophomore boy whose head is on a whirl
just because of a junior girl
the junior girl in her sleek black sedan
persistently pursues a senior man
the senior man so dashing and wild
is hopelessly in love with the freshman child

Patricia Wynn is from Eatonton, Ga. When shes not scrolling through Tumblr, shes usually writing. Currently 19, Patricia plans to be a published author by 25.
Allpoetry.com/Patricia_Wynn

[Sally M. Clark]

He was my home

Five years have elapsed
since two kindred aliens
crossed paths.

2014 May
that voice
an untitled track
favorited
eons ago
locked on repeat.

She was a golden child
surrounded by popular lemmings
perpetual solitude
too terrified
to wear her weird.

She found
in him
a finally
first familiar soul.

He revered her,
magnanimous
as she unraveled.
Gut-shredding
skin-crawling

debilitating anxiety
descents to hell
glass-eyed
major depressive disorder.

He was enthralled
by her myriad of eccentricities
fire and ice
fanaticism
for art
poetry
all things handmade
imperfect roadside antiques.

Her veritable high
upon the discovery
of a first-edition
hardback
intoxicatingly aromatic
yellowed, brittle pages
1950-something
tattered and faded cover
embellished with gold lettering
in perfect cursive
on the tattering spine.

Seamlessly, ceaselessly
he navigated
a parlous hinterland
she had devised
hiding

sacred shameful contents
painstakingly camouflaged
singed trappings of a soul.

Calmly and confidently
he sidestepped
land mines
covert
uncharted
intuition his guide.

Steadily, skillfully
he sliced
through razor-tipped brambles,
carving a path
towards her hell.
Unequivocally sacred
sonorously loathsome
foreclosed
decrepit
long-since inhabited.

Barn wood door
rusted machete
revelation
jagged jewel tones

Ungloved hands
usurped
rich hues
daggers and scalpels

applied a viscous
lead reduction
reframed
repurposed
unrecognized beauty
within her soul.

Arcane sanctuary
carpentered for her:
singular stained-glass window
source of sunlight.

A tornado
uninvited suspiration
venerated and resurrected
just long enough
to precariously
eviscerate and slice,
precariously turning on
all of the lights
she had extinguished
after five years of waiting for
"Come home, babe."

Sally resides in Birmingham, Alabama.
Pain is the pen that purges my past and carves a path towards
the promise of a tomorrow. Allpoetry.com/smc

[Lisa F. Raines]
haiku - grey morning

clouds have descended

caught like cotton on the pines

steamy fog thickens

AlisRamie is from North Carolina, USA.
Interests include: philosophy, history, international relations,
poetry, art, design, jazz, funk, and some good old soul.
Allpoetry.com/AlisRamie

[Janet and Eugene Ballone]

[seashells grace the shore]

seashells grace the shore

as glistening objects hide

mother of fine pearls

Janet Ballone is from New Jersey, USA. She is a self published author of two books, 'Poems of the Soul' and 'The Woodman' which is a children's fairy tale about bullying. Allpoetry.com/Jan_Serene

[Rs Cobb]

Night of Sirens

The hood doesn't sleep night
People might take your life
And they won't twice
If you are alone at night
I pray that you be alright

Liquor cases and kush ashes
Caressing the cellulite,
Is boss hands on lesbian asses

As the world spins
Like a Frisbee
being tossed in between two hands
Dangles the life of friend

Son, mother, daughter
Aunt, cousin, nephew
Pitiful tears,
Falling like waterfalls
That no one can hear

Bodies on top of bodies
Sponsored by the racks on racks on racks
In the hood
But dropping bombs
Like we in Baghdad

Amen,
Pray to
whatever deity watches over you
Look up
to See the ghetto bird watching you

Lights, camera, action
Bullet sounds
is something you grow a custom to
Warning shots sound like fireworks
So hit the deck because they coming for you

Young black youths living life by the barrel
Hood pirates
Pull up on like Captain Jack Sparrow

Candle light visuals we need a moment silence
It's the night of sirens

A writer and poet from California, Raymond is currently earning his Bachelor's degree. He has published six books, and currently working on his seventh. Follow him on instagram @mindthetypos Allpoetry.com/R._S._Cobb

[Sean Mitchell]

That H-Town Sound

Hello and welcome to the H-Town sound.
Delivered to you like an Astros fastball from the pitcher's
mound.
I don' know whether it's square or round,
But this city has it all, where people of all races abound.

Get past traffic and into the fast lane,
You'll rarely see much profane.
You'll rarely see horses or cows
But instead an urban cosmopolitan that makes you say "wow."

It's that H-Town sound.

Sean Mitchell is a writer, poet, journalist and photographer
from the Houston area. He enjoys sports, especially college
basketball, and learning. Allpoetry.com/SeanMitchell

[Lorri Ventura]

Two Tigers

Circling each other warily
Two tigers
In a cage built of
Deceit and grudges
Blowing on the embers
Of a union reduced to
An emotional junk drawer
Rifling through
Expired passion and broken communication
Clutching at sweetly scented memories
Apart together
Unhappily married couple

Lorri Ventura is a retired special education administrator living in Massachusetts. She is new to poetry-writing. Allpoetry.com/Lorri_Ventura

[Dawn Mueller]
Something Other

In the same way I
know how to breathe
and when,
my body remembers
your swaddled
contours.

The slight weight
of your perfect fit
in the strange cradle
of me-
a symmetry of needs
sated,   the way
thirst meets water.

The unexpected
glorious shock of you,
like a levee's breech-
unhinged; expanded me
far past the yield point-
my old shape
cast forever aside.

Your fresh, new skin's glow
dwarfed the sun
those quiet, miraculous
nights I revolved

around your form
in pure awe

becoming
something other.
A thing fiercer
and softer, something
fuller and stronger -
I became
yours.

Dawn Mueller is from Southern Illinois, where she lives with
her husband of 29 years and two youngest of six children. She
has been writing poetry for 2 years.
Allpoetry.com/Dawn_Mueller

[Stephen Hollins]

in blind faith

a blindfolded, bald, quadriplegic acorn
lives underground, a beggar of the earth
with no money or letters to his name
or even a signature to mark himself

his only companion an eyeless, speechless worm
ok perhaps an occasional frantic mole
no day or night bag, no baggage at all
but a little crown upon his head, his only jewel
not a drop of light or a moons eclipse
nor a fiddler, organist, singer or preachers hope

no tigers, kings, horses or flying children
his cloak stitched in darkness

the watchmaker's ax splits
this minstrel's dark brown back
exposing a creamy wrinkled flesh
his finger shafts into the wet soil

as another skyward arises
standing over fallen leaves
unfolds his tiny hands
to the golden syrup of the sun

Dacians, Celts, Romans called the Oak
'the tree of the Gods'

strength and endurance
spans a thousand years and more

exercised as an oracle, a tonic,
to heal scarring, disinfecting, tissue fortifier
hemorrhoids, gingivitis, frostbite, sweating
harnessed in shipbuilding, wine barrels
furniture, flooring for kings to paupers

grandfather poet
of blind faith
grows a secret conviction
in the jewel of his crown

I am loving writing poetry I live on Waiheke Island New
Zealand. I specialize in Improv for Theatre, Acting,
Storytelling, Dance, Clown, Mime, Teaching, Building.
Allpoetry.com/Stephen_Hollins

[Michael Camacho]

When is it poem when is it song

bones rolling
down the hill
The sight stills
the mind chills
caught in a lake
filled with tears
In anguish
the yells of curdling shrills

birds now shapes
with thin groans
beaks shattered
scrape at the floor
doors slam
they won't anymore
who are to blame
when killing the tree
wont change
dont thing

they break under its gaze
and shapes well
with smell
and decay
things of joy
lost in noise
The terrible drill

be still in my throat

The fourth has lost
winding of light
receding of growth
and shied delight
streatching so far
to still the weight
in become
something not fate

Michael.n0n lives in Anthem Arizona. It writes because,
madness is not fun, so the paper must catch it.
Allpoetry.com/Michael.n0n

[Cynthia Morphew]

Hidden Lies

Marriage can be a dark closet
closed to the light
Once opened
shelves are empty
The clothes an unfamiliar smell
deep within the corners
Lay the secrets
never meant to be unveiled

My poetry is the way I connect with real life events of my
own. It's easier to write it down, then say out loud.
Allpoetry.com/Abby_Lane

[Eugenia Fain]

Autumn

Fall leaves tumble down

Filling bags all over town

Get the rake-Let's go

I am from Columbia, South Carolina. I live with my husband Ivan and tabby cat Buddy. I have been publishing since age eleven and am an Amazon author. I have written longer fiction, short stories . Allpoetry.com/Mywife304

[Joey Uzar]

Scary Man Down The Street

The Scary Man Down The Street
Thin fingers, bulging eyes,
Rib cage showing, teeth long and pointy,
Looks all scary and not so hairy.
Horns all sharp that are shaped like a harp,
Feet all furry and very dirty.
Has no nose, but his eyes glow.
Stalking around from tree to tree making animals all flee,
Screeching and moaning through the night,
Causing millions to fright,
As it walks on all fours
Scratching on the door.
Feasting on flesh is what this carnivore does best.
Crawling into your houses
Eating ALL of your mouses!
As he stalks around for his food, he is also nude.
He crawls through the night, giving people screams of fright.
However, don't ever turn on your light unless you want to die
tonight.
Stay in your houses and save all your mouses
For this humanoid crawls through the night.

DinoHun is a young kid. Just starting out and this is my very
first poem. I hope you enjoy it. Writing poems is a release of
stress and a fulfillment of joy into my heart.
Allpoetry.com/DinoHun

[Aamer Khan]

Glass love

Love has left me empty.
It has turned me into
glass.
Run a wet finger around
me
and you'll hear my hollow
scream.
I am shatter.
Fragile.
Just the right pitch
and you will
break me.
Drop me and you'll see
what I am.
Shards of a man.
Broken.

There is little to say about Viktor. He's a simple man who writes nonsense when he's got nothing to do or when he runs out of cigarettes. Allpoetry.com/Viktor_K

[Joanne Tolles]

Songbirds Singing Alone

Trapped in the grasp of the red branch
Hidden from the blazing sun
Enwrapped in the stillness of the night

The songbirds wait.

Severed from the life behind the clouds
Startled by the raging pulse of the red sap
of the Dragon Tree
Silent in anticipation of the coming storm

The songbirds reach out to each other.

Separated by the winds and the night flares
Seeking shelter and warmth in each other's wings
Dashed into the grasping arms of the Dragon Tree

The songbirds shudder.

Why did they not plan?
Why did they not stay as one?
Why did they allow the promise of the Spring Goddess
to instill hope of new life?

The songbirds brave the storm alone
Waiting, reaching out, and shuddering
Until the storm passes

194

And the Spring Goddess breaks forth
And life is renewed and joy returns.

And the songbirds sing sweet melodies.

I am a wife, step-mom, grandma, and alpha female to two
fabulous canines and one very verbal kitty cat. I teach high
school English in real-life and am an education activist and
SJS survivor. Allpoetry.com/thelordreigns

[Alwyn Barddylbach]

Chorus of a Thousand Dreams

The universe is
glorious, hallow and quiet,
unrestrained like you and I
in the stillness gathered

while you sleep
it hums your woeful tune,
its followers weep in
the storm of a noble heart

we the multitude,
the silent belly
swallow its humble beat
mindful of your part

as a thief of darkness thrives.

I wrestle with sadness,
this restless face stares
back at the bones of an
angry moon

for I cannot know your
anguish, your solitude
where the madness of
a lonely dark cloud lies

I cannot know how
living hours languish
on the emptiness of days,
death of endless ways

years that had barely begun.

And I remember them,
the magnitude of our
tomorrows, the scope
of things to come

I learnt to think and swim,
trust my part, reach out
and touch the searing edge
of an old Siberian sun

every dream we caught
every smile we gave
every breath we saved
that glacial moment lingers

it melts on a poet's tongue.

Chorus of a thousand
suns stir softly, loveless
joyful dare, all
fingers to the flames

the universe is
deep with tranquil pulse

spirals brim and
inhospitable shadows

every night must end
every winter broken
every morning borrowed
in the stillness gathered

while we hum this woeful tune.

———————————

Look up at the night sky it's swimming with them. Song to the
sun, where all our troubles may be longingly forgotten –
Aussie Quatrain AB, Blue Mountains.
Allpoetry.com/Barddylbach

[Jemma M]

Ragamuffin

Ragamuffin, ragamuffin
Dreaming of perfection

Laze until late in the day
Hair, brain, mind, all burnt hay

Cry until eyes become red and puffy
Secluded in bed: safe, warm and fluffy

Sulk and sleep
Wallow and weep
Smoke and drink
Ruminate and think

Performing required chores of each day
Leaving no time or desire to play

Wine and whine
Depression divine

Ragamuffin, ragamuffin
Ya ain't got nothin'

Jemma M is from Vancouver, BC. Poetry is the best therapy for my life. I'm always open to the journey of learning, guidance, and improvement. Allpoetry.com/Jemma_M

[Stephen Hollins]

velvet for the blind to touch

two decades have passed
the whisper of grey curtains
drawn silence over Lady Diana
Princess of Wales

arisen to the glossy pages of
'the peoples' queen of fashion'
primrose flowered gem
painted in a sunny English garden

from shy Di, wearing
pie-crust blouses, pastel ruffles
to a blossoming groomed woman
striding in gowns and body-con red velvet
this world's most-photographed women

Diana's wedding dress
closely guarded secret
in fashions history

ivory taffeta frilled lace gown
a 25-foot train 153-yard tulle veil
fabric spun on a British silk farm
hand embroidered with sequins

a small blue bow is sewn into the waistband
10,000 pearls and Carrickmacross lace insert

that once belonged to Queen Mary
for luck an 18-carat gold trinket horseshoe charm
studded with white diamonds attached to the label

crowned with the Spencer family tiara
an 18th century-era heirloom
silk shoes, covered in 542 sequins and 132 pearls
completed with a scent of Quelques Fleurs
perfume sprayed on her dress

Is she the best-dressed women in history?
Audrey Hepburn and Jackie Kennedy
stand in her shadow of flashing cameras
her style so mirrored and adored

she spoke with her clothing
through the novel costumes she wore
a starry palace style for traveling abroad
weaving and waving fabrics diplomacy flag

attire saluting the host country
dress emblazoned with gold falcons
an emblem of Saudi Arabia

her care giving wardrobe stimulates
cheerful colorful presence in hospitals
reachable and warm ungloved hands
chunky colorful jewelry for children
'You can't cuddle a child while wearing a hat.'

velvet for the blind to touch
dressing naked skin
to massage the heartbeat
of herself and the world.

I am loving writing poetry I live on Waiheke Island New
Zealand. I specialize in Improv for Theatre, Acting,
Storytelling, Dance, Clown, Mime, Teaching, Building.
Allpoetry.com/Stephen_Hollins

[Lacy Rostyak]

Let Me..

walk up slowly
speak to me softly
take my hands
and take me away
let me
take you away
lovely and slowly.
let me...

look up slowly
whisper to me softly
take my body
and take me away
let me
take you away
sweetly and slowly
let me...

_____

A musician: born in the rural south - raised in the city.
Lacy has been writing poems, songs, and short stories since
the first day her mom gave her a journal on her 6th birthday.
Allpoetry.com/CountryLace

[Stephanie Jane O'hanlon]

Euphonic

How perfectly disordered,
The vibrato of life, in harmony.
The springs, of lamb & daffodil,
The sacred scents of splendour, still.
The dawn of this avian chorus is humming,
Beneath hives of honeyed harps, strumming.
The angels adorn the melodies of April,
As heaven's tapestry embroiders earth,
The alchemy of the universe in rebirth.
Love blossoms with admiration,
Kissing the miracles of divinity,
With the lips of ripe creation.

I have a heart of ink & a passion for poetry, conceptual art & photography. I'm a proud mother & doting dog lover. I live in Liverpool in the UK. I truly believe that Equality lies in Diversity.

Allpoetry.com/Heart_of_Ink

[Alinda Daniels]

The Bus Stop

School days, school days ... It's that time of year
Up bright and early, the bus is almost here.
Wiping the sleep from my eyes, I soon can see
God granted my wish - some sunshine for me.

Greeted by my pal - You know Captain Crunch,
We sit down for breakfast, I like him a bunch!
Hurry to the dresser to comb and brush my hair;
Got to be ready 'cause the bus will soon be there.

Mama's in the kitchen, daddy's gone to work.
Little brother is mama's shadow, tugging at her skirt.
Not quite ready to spread his wings and fly,
I whisper "I love you" then hug and kiss goodbye.

Out the door, down the road, I'm off to meet the bus.
Kicking at the pebbles and stirring up some dust,
Waiting and looking as far as I can see,
Look! Here comes the bus - coming just for me.

Alinda is from a small town in South Carolina. Retired grandmother with two wonderful children, one in Heaven and another close by. Proud of one grandson and one great grandbaby. Allpoetry.com/Adnls1948

[Lorri Ventura]

Domestic Violence

Daddy shot the family dog
Because it looked at him the wrong way
Mommy's ribs
Like two rows of broken wishbones
In the x-ray

Shut up, little girl
And swallow the Benadryl
So you can sleep through the yelling
Fifty-five years later
Oral meds still taste like terror and rage

Those are just baby teeth
It's okay that Daddy knocked them out
You'll grow new ones
And he had a rough day at work
Poor Daddy

Daddy's handgun lived on the hutch
Always oiled
Always loaded
Often brandished in our faces
To keep us in our places

Pray, sweet child of mine, Mommy said, You are my angel
Daddies can't kill angels
They just like to try

The little girl refused to pray to a God
Who sees without helping

Lorri Ventura is a retired special education administrator
living in Massachusetts. She is new to poetry-writing.
Allpoetry.com/Lorri_Ventura

[Mara TreviñO]

Steady Sun

A detonating silence,
that stutters through time
relentlessly navigating forward
with a firm hand

Easy does it
is a spell of the mind
to embrace the darkness of the void,
an avid disciple of the eternal blank

Ever-changing chameleon,
rising above ambiguity
an insidious conquest,
determined to obliterate the gloaming
locked in motion
rather than chambers

Intricately bewitched,
in a trance she knows
steady, steady, steady
she goes

Mara is from Monterrey, México. Poetry is my very pulse, my
only constant. I wear it around my neck like a medal.
Allpoetry.com/Mara_stf

[Janice Mathis]

The Delusion of Permanence

nothing in our lives remain the same
the only constant is constant change
people come and people go
the winds of time shift and blow

scattering our dreams with one breath
leaving only ashes, pain and death
clearing the slate to begin anew
foundations laid, the delusions grew

structures built by grandiose design
crumble into the sifting sands of time
limitless time bears witness to confusion
permanence is naught but a grand illusion.

Janice is a wife, proud mother and grandmother. She has
always enjoyed poetry and has recently rediscovered her joy
in writing. Allpoetry.com/GypsyLady13

[Eric James Allred Porter]

The Tale of the Eluthanai

Deep in the mine Eluthanai work
Demonic masters offer them no shirk
But light of Flame is burning bright
Gives hope for them, freedom's plight

And in their souls reflects the Flame
The world above, it sets their aim
Will of their own, it doth bestow
From dungeon deep, down below

To stand up to oppression's hand
With solid trust they form their band
The Flame it shows their path to go
To demon's castle in the snow

And to the Flame, they pray for aid
It hears their call, their cries are bade
With Flame in hand, against the sword
They stand against their Demon Lord

Up from the cave, the workers burst
To keep of Lord, the Flame leads first
By light of Flame, they break his power
They throw their Lord from the tower

Eric Porter is from Orem, UT where he lives with his husband, and cat Beans. In my free time I like to write and play Dungeons & Dragons. Allpoetry.com/Eric_Porter

[Duncan Wagner]

Oil Change 3

"The Boss backs you up"
Yes, I'm sure that she does

Chrome interspersed with an odd green
How it must be hell to work here

which is not there, never there
This static room, florescent and cruel

Sterile at the dawn of feeling ripped off
Perhaps there's a better way of tasting this contempt

I feel alien in this unchanged internal combustion world
They sell snowplows I'd never buy

These Winesburg thieves
How they've conned the entire community

Yet I must transact here
The scamming scam-miesters of upper Sarasota

How I long for my past life
as Cleopatra's personal charioteer

This place has nothing to offer
I can't wait to leave

can't wait for something else

just outside this frosted nothingness
just outside the extra titanium and reinforced doors

Duncan Wagner is from Sarasota Florida. Poetry has become
my obsession. I have many basement projects underway.
Spring is coming. Yayyyyyyyy!
Allpoetry.com/Duncan_Wagner

[Stephanie Downes]

For the Love of Apollo

To be a wild pink rose kissed by the Sun

That's what I'd be

In a garden lit with purest gold

Untouched by the bitter cold

The walks with creepers overrun

Growing free.

———————————

I am from Chester, UK. Poetry for me is a safety valve for when I get too full of words. I have a degree in English & Creative Writing, and sometimes it even shows.
Allpoetry.com/RoseaLupum

[Patricia Marie Batteate]
Food for Fought

It started with a single olive; it bounced right off his head
Like a game of tag, my turn, he threw a loaf of bread

Soon the others joined, and the fight was going strong
Mash potatoes, green beans, even Filet Mignon

Apple pie and ice cream, both went flying by
A bombarding of mixed nuts, nearly caught my eye

There were Hamburgers, baked Alaska, even egg foo young
Like a tornado hitting a drive-thru, this place was really spun

It was everyone for themselves, or be a sitting duck
It started out as a formal dinner, now turned potluck

This went on for hours, not a truce was called
If Sara Lee were here, I was the one she mauled

Finally the war had ended, and what a sight to see
Food caked everywhere, in the wall, a can of peas

We all pitched in together, for hours on our feet
At last a chance to rest, is there anything to eat?

I am a 7th generation Californian. I am an engineer, poet and
artist. I could see poets inheriting the earth.
Allpoetry.com/Patricia_Marie

[Sharon Mooney]

A charming elderly couple

Her hand lightly on his chest
his lifeline holding her
for a few pressing days.
They both know the time.
Seven decades of fusing into one
now ready to be cleaved apart
with one exhale.

Women survive their husband's death
he whispers broken and hushed
But men cannot continue on!
His deep ache crushing
his ribs, battering his future
they are not afraid, they are breaking.
She is already separating.

Held, her hand will guide him
to stand with her at the threshold
repeating their lifelong pattern.
Much to ready before they kiss
she too fears he may not recover
but it matters not quite so much
her eye drawn to new horizon.

She begins to see they will continue
with only a delicate line between
where she is and he is not

She has readied, he cannot.
Her eye longing for crisp azure sky
her heart bent to the wild horizon
her pulse senses freedom.

I have been writing for more than 35 years. It is a life stream of mine. I live on the Sea of Cortez in northern Mexico. Aging, death & the spirit of life are repeating topics in my prose and poetry. Allpoetry.com/WriteMexico

[Autumn Shirley]

Power

through the dark
you will find
the light that shines bright
in all his glory
with all his might
JESUS
will take away your fright
with JESUS you will
survive

JESUS has been my inspiration through my entire life,
through my trails of life i have learned to become a better soul
full of love and inspiration that i can share with the world.
Allpoetry.com/faithful_lamb

[Lisa F. Raines]

Haiku - Impressions

tumultuous thoughts

as I walk on an island

footprints washed away

AlisRamie is from North Carolina, USA.
Interests include: philosophy, history, international relations,
poetry, art, design, jazz, funk, and some good old soul.
Allpoetry.com/AlisRamie

[Vernoica Thibodeaux]

The Love Letter

Looking in the moonlight,
A silhouette, curvaceous and seductive,
With touch as soft as wind.
Eyes of fire; a semblance of uncanny speak

With every word,
the strong becomes submissive
The wild, becomes tame.

Eyes controlling everything,
you hold dear.
Revealing secrets,
only for the grave.

Flesh leave bones,
when she is not near
to caress them
with pain and sickness

My mind says to leave,
but I need her like a drug
that make me everything,
but also no one

Proud as a lion roaming wild,
there is no one like her
In all the kingdoms

This is a love letter written to me by my husband and greatest admirer Wilton Thibodeaux. I am his Muse, but he has brought the greatest poetry to my life
Allpoetry.com/Vernoica

[Antoinette Mier-Rosales]

Hyperion and Helios

Perpetual pursuit in reach of the sky
Need of the all to understand the why

Seeds planted never faltering to rest
Germinate to blossom in synthesis

Encircling rings within a tree
Reflecting solitarily

Photograph in contrast to Jamais Vu
Oppose all allowed and revealed to you

Branching onwards like elec-tri-city
Paying attention to 9 6 and 3

Forced to ignite instruction never to burn
Hover above awaiting eternal return

Primordial roots already in place
Attempt to unearth my own true face

KRONOS cited 3 6 and 9
Hungering time to taste the divine

Manifesting Intent - Transcend Destiny
Eyes Perceiving - Ascend Synchronicity

Where does the I start?
Where does the I end?

Kaleidoscope MIND - Vessel to BEND.

———————————————

If my fragment of expression were to reach only one on a journey through night into the light of the Sun is a wish come true. Allpoetry.com/Hypnos

[Maria Schembri]

Angels Are Amongst Us

Angels are amongst us
Angels all around
If we quiet our minds, and open our hearts
We will hear their heavenly sound

Angels do protect us
Sent from our Father up above
To guide us along in this confusing world
With reassurance and love

Everyone has an angel
Given to us from the start
Trust and faith is what we need
To hear them in our heart

Never feel alone or scared
desolate or sad
For when we feel these things at times
Our angels do take charge

They comfort us with an enveloping hug
Making sure we know they are there
They only want the best for us
Because they really truly care.

MSchembri is from Toronto area, and loves to write poetry in her spare time when she is not volunteering.
Allpoetry.com/MSchembri

[Ishara Das]

Lost, Yet Found!

Lost in woods, I walk alone,
In the only path that can be found.
My shadow follows me through it all,
But I don't feel alone or don't feel scared-
like a single willow standing in a storm.
I march through feeling content, feeling strong,
I march through like a single willow standing in the storm.

Darkness falls, my shadow escapes,
I look around for a single space-
where I can sit and think it through;
looking for an escape to my solace-
I look for a clue.

Alone there I feel so strong,
I look up, stand and march along.
No one to say me where to go-
No one to say me where I belong.
I belong to me and no one else;
I belong to me and my respect.

In the opening ahead I see my loved ones stand-
I feel scared, turn around and ran...
Lost again in the woods, but now I am strong,
Lost again in the woods, but I am not alone.

InkkedSolace is from my heart. I ink down what I am feeling at that moment. I write my mind and heart.
Allpoetry.com/Inkkedsolace

[J. Tanner Snow]

The Lying Angel's Song

Ambience of dread and suppression, keeping them in their graves.
The little animals skitter over the ghosts of meadows that were,
Weeping for the losses of the good gods that they once craved.
At what point must they stop to see that good and evil concur?
In any case, they'll bleed under leaders who are in turn enslaved
To the endless drive to initiate the end, for him or for her.

Laboring all day, dying in the sun, all so you can drive
The hated memories into the flimsy vault we built long ago.
So go on spilling your soul over death. Go on whispering your lies.
If there is a silver lining to this, you'll never let yourself know.
For the serenity and suffering, you're not long to remain alive
In this twisted, ruined world we've come to call Syl-No.

And thus within the crimson light this stage is set
Beneath the eyes of a sadistic watcher suspended above.
Mindless puppets wielding the blades for those forever unmet;
Banging their fists into the pitted walls marked with love;
Clamping the gun between their teeth at the black Angel's behest.

My scarred liars, it's time to clip the wings of the Dove.

———————————

J. Tanner Snow is an entity, probably not of this Earth. No one knows why exactly it writes poetry, but considering the ambiguous nature of it's being there's probably not a very comforting reason. Allpoetry.com/Xaire

[Bradley Driskill]

I Am

One lost lamb led astray,
Legion who dwelled in him cast away.
Back to the abyss transported by the swine,
Christ made it worth leaving the ninety nine.

The blind now see
Prisoners of demons set free.
Life restored to the dead,
As Jairus's daughter awakes from her bed.

Adulteress whose sins were many
Forgiven, for her love to Him was plenty.
Lepers on the verge of decay
Made clean for they know He's the only way.

For saving grace had walked the earth,
To give us who face death a second birth.
Our souls He didn't come to damn,
Praise our Lord Jesus the great I AM.

———————————

Bradley Driskill is from Spout Spring, Va. He writes poetry to
show his love for Jesus Christ and hope's it leads others to
Him. Bradley is also happily married to his wife Christen.
Allpoetry.com/Bradley_Driskill

[Lisa F. Raines]

We cry blood, not tears

Our pores exude hope,
not sweat

We drink love

Writers weep war
Artists bleed rainbows

Poets eat inspiration

Politicians excrete positions
Lawyers regurgitate the law

Musicians swim in beauty,
the luckiest of us all!

AlisRamie is from North Carolina, USA.
Interests include: philosophy, history, international relations,
poetry, art, design, jazz, funk, and some good old soul.
Allpoetry.com/AlisRamie

[Shanna Tognarelli]

Miss Perfect Queen

What part of me shall I show them? What role shall I play?
I can be anyone I want to be. I'll be someone else today.

They will think that I am confident. That I'm funny. That I'm
smart
No one will ever know what's Inside of the depths of my
heart.

Can I persuade them into thinking, that I'm someone to love?
When I feel I am a little bit, a bit less than enough.

Can I hide all of my shyness? Can I mask all of my pain?
Refer to me as your highness. I'm the miss perfect queen.

Because my eyes are just the brightest, out of all of those
you've seen.
And my life is just perfection. I am living the dream.

I have a perfect face and my body is just right.
If you think that I am the kindest, then I'm doing all right.

How long will I play this part and how many lies can I tell?
Ask me how I'm doing because I'm always doing well.

How long can I pretend to be, somebody that I'm not?
Until Shanna is just another random name that they forgot.

I must now let go of this facade because if I don't, I fear.
If I don't chose to stand up tall, I'll fall so far Ill disappear.

Hello my name is Shanna and I think it is essential, that you
know that just like you, I am unique and truly special.

My name is Shanna Tognarelli. I'm a 37 year old women from
the state of Massachussettes. Some of my poetry is a bit dark
like my favorite poet, Quoth the Raven Nevermore. Poe
was/is a huge inspiration Allpoetry.com/Imperfectgirl

[Catherine Jean Lindsey Towery Sales]

Dressed like a Queen

Dressed today as if I were the Queen
Wearing your Beautiful Colors so Well
Be Loyal to your Rich Regal Past
Sharing your history so it will last

with Fabrics so Fabulous
yes Red, Purple and Blue
Sharing these Fabrics
will often Tell
I'm worthy to be called a Queen
With or Without a King

My Heritage has Surpass
some of the most awful deeds
Hatred, Bitterness, Injustice, and Inequalities
just because of the Color or my Skin

Why do I have to Struggle to be Free
No more, no more will you Confine me
I'm Dressing like a Queen
For the entire world to see
Not for you it's really for me
My reason to Dress is to Impress
I will continue to Dress for Success
Why? Cause I am a Queen

Worthy of R.E.S.P.E.C.T and to be Seen

in Fabrics of Golden Threads
Heck I may even wear my Dreads
Designed to Drape my Hips, Shoulders and Head
Adoring my body with Regal Designs
What gives you the Audacity to Define
Just because I like being Divine
I will continue to Dress to Impress

My Royal Heritage of Indian, African,
yes Even White
that's just a Color of my skin
but it doesn't define Who I am,
I wear clothes that makes
me feel good

Boosting my Ego and
my Self Esteem
Yes to me is the way
it all seems
A Style so Unique
Keeps Me in a
Positive mood
Heck, I know that
I look Good

Some may Say
where is your King
My King doesn't define
me or my history
no one can make me sad
or blue

I'm dressed to Impress
Yes even the likes of you

In Red, Black, Purple and Blue
with braids, curls, and these jewels
yes of course they match my shoes
you can't take away my Crown
Wherever I step its
on Holy Ground

Grooming my Image with
a Style to Impress
I will continue to dress my best
and Know I won't settle
for anything Less
I am worthy to be
called a Queen
Invest in self and
only the Best

My mind, body and my spirit
Heals my health giving me wealth
I will continue to look my best
No, I won't Settle
for anything less
I am Dressed Like a Queen

Catherine Sales is a former Ed Counselor from Compton,
CA.She holds several Master Degrees in Psychology,
Education, Human Behavior, & Education Adm. Cred.
Former President PA4C M.H .Advocacy 501C.
Allpoetry.com/Cathy_salesmft

[Leleca Knohoff]

An Open Book

One day, I opened a book
Started to read,
Here it is My life,
I kept on reading and saw all
that had happened to me in the past

Scared I continued, to read parts of my present life
Wow I said; how exciting this is
My life IS an open book, I want to know more
As I turned the page, shaking and longing to know the rest.
A thought came to mind
Maybe I should just have a peek

I knew the rest of my life had been written there,
That I knew.
joy would fill my heart,
And deception come to the point of killing me

Trying to suppress my curiosity
I held the pages tightly, and then heard,,,,,
NO, this part of the book is not to be opened
Live it instead.

Leleca Knohoff from Sunny Florida, born on another country
on earth, through the way of Ny, S.C. to Florida Deep
Feelings and thoughts unfold and I just pen it
Allpoetry.com/Toowindy4me

[Andrew Lee Joyner]
Emotionally scarred

Marks on the body seen with a story,
Thoughts in mind, heard but not seen
To erase the impact is definitely hard
As the scars increase on yourself
Emotions flow deep within oneself
Leaving a path of a twisted past
Try as you might it's always in vain,
To let memories go can take a lifetime
So sad but too true, try to find your way
As you gain more memories everyday
Whether self inflicted or not they are there to stay, emotional
scars that won't go away...

When i started writing it became a hobby of mine and now in
the long run It's become a goal . I love to read and write; my
inspiration comes from events i may encounter.
Allpoetry.com/Andrew_lee

[Curtis Lee Turner Jr.]
2300 Miles To The West

6 hours by Plane
48 hours by Train
35 hours by Car
Our feelings are
Still close, but
Distance told Reality it's
just too far.

700 hours by feet, and 30 days, without a
Good night sleep. 4 days by postal mail
2 weeks, If I let the wind, hit the sail.

Wishing I could see you, soon, It's impossible to be there,
by a hot air balloon.

3 to 5 seconds to connect by cellphone
And, 365 days are sadly gone,
60 seconds by email, 2300 miles,
Away, time has spoken, with a lot to say.

Thewriterc lives in Columbus, Ohio writing since the age of
12 years old. Songs, commercials jingles, and working on my
screenplay for films. I believe poetry is born in the heart and
mind. Allpoetry.com/Thewriterc

[Joseph Faucault]

My Sweet Sunshine

The day we met, I never knew
That I would fall in love with you.

Your smile, your wit, your style and grace
You'd have stood still, in my place.

We've had our times, good and bad,
We've had our times, happy and sad.

But now we know, that when it comes time,
We will always agree, YOU ARE MY SUNSHINE!!!

Joseph Faucault is originally from Chicago, Ill. Moved to
Denver, CO, and now resides in Sierra Vista, AZ. 39.7559*N,
104.9942*W, these numbers have a special meaning to me,
and this poem. Allpoetry.com/Joseph_Faucault

[Michael Flanary]

My drug

You pull me into your arms for a hug
Tonight, your kisses will be my drug
Like a junkie I am hooked on you
And I'll be flying after a kiss or two

I'm enchanted by your sweet lips
Begging for just one more sip
One more taste of heavenly bliss
I'm intoxicated by every single kiss

_____

Michael Flanary was born in Louisville, KY and raised in
Memphis, TN. He served in the Air Force for 22 years and
currently lives in Norman, OK Allpoetry.com/mflanary

[Shane Ali]

Across the Sea

Stranger
In a foreign land,
How did you find me
In this vast unplanned?

Ever moving
Across the sea,
A blissful distance
Our melancholy.
From that place
Far away,
We share our words
To meet one day.

Let's fight the tide,
Just a pond for us,
An Insignificance...
I'll skip across.

Time, norms,
Expectations,
All meaningless
Fabrications.

I'll come to you
In the great immense,
For our moment

To reveal
Fate's intent.

I'll be there soon.
Wait for me,
In your distant place
Across the sea.

For M.P. If only we could will ourselves to meet, despite the distance and life's walls. Your energy is with me as I wait for you. See you soon. Allpoetry.com/Shane_Ali

[Curtis Lee Turner Jr.]
When will you miss me

When will you miss me, I'm just curious to know
Perhaps in the winter, the first sight of snow, or after dinner
when his love struggles to show.

Will you miss me when violets grow blue, and your having
thoughts
of her loving me too.

Could it happen, when the leaves change colors, and you
realize
You will never love another, I'm just curious to know.
Maybe I'm just a house, and not a home, nothing permanent,
just a high-interest loan. Or I'm like rain in it's purest form,
evaporating before hitting the surface, because my love was
too warm.

Thewriterc lives in Columbus, Ohio writing since the age of
12 years old. Songs, commercials jingles, and working on my
screenplay for films. I believe poetry is born in the heart and
mind.

Allpoetry.com/Thewriterc

[Nicole a. Hawley]

Belisama

Celtic Goddess of Lakes and Rivers, Fire, Crafts and Light

I am from the forest,
gravel path, tunnel of twisted branches
decaying wood stumps.
Stench of dead earth.
Mucky, stale moss-filmed swamps.
Bullfrogs croak.
Goose droppings.
Crickets chirp.

I am from the darkness,
traveling that endless gravel path.
Where are you light?
I search for you.
My truth lives there.
I only see you — round eyes, dimples.
Man in the moon far out of reach.

I am from that blustering wind.
Pushes against my back.
Strikes my face.
Carries me to where I need to be.
Am I getting any closer,
to my tranquility?
Keep running.

I am from the hope where dreams flourish.

Is there a better road,
for destiny to follow?
My compass broken.
Meant for so much more.
Must find where true aspirations take shape.
Is there such a place?

I am from the sun,
his sweet rays not warm my bitter heart.
Endless day?
Final hour?
Both, weight of boulder resting atop my shoulders.
So heavy a carry.
One foot in front of the other.
Lead the way.

I am from that which has no name,
for I bleed.
Bloody screams!
Throat clenched.
Do you not hear me?
Echoes carry, but High Fathers you turn.
Walk away.
You, my ignorance and betrayal.

I am from the water,
whose rhythmic current grants me balance.
Place I go to achieve my enigmatic calm.
Draws me in.
Only feels right that I follow.
Addicted to its refreshing bliss.

246

Clothes my nude vulnerabilities.
Such serenity.

I am from the out-stretched limb,
it lies across that gravel path.
I methodically travel.
No part of any plan.
YOU made me stumble and fall!
Through tears,
I see your hand gently reach for mine.
Rise!

I am from my companions,
hands clasped, they travel alongside me.
Otherwise my journey fruitless.
May I come with you?
Not sure how to answer.
I have no confirmed destination.
Continue moving then.
Let's run!

I am from potion of innocence naivety created,
conjured by the Devil.
Sick, twisted games.
Fool I was!
Believed I had the Angel sent by Hosanna.
Instead struck by truth's alarm.
by evil's mighty anvil.

I am from the chaos,
of which Man created so that he may dwell.

Fear, my hell now.
Black veil masks the misery.
Spirit frozen.
Silenced.
Friends, I cry out.
You no longer wish to stay.

I am from the burning torch,
that rejuvenates my inner flame.
Those who always believed.
They carry and remain.
Hitting rock bottom.
What become of your heart now, woman?
Guarded.
Who could blame?

I am from the book of wisdom and knowledge,
now forced to read.
He and others before.
Ate my soul.
Buried the bones.
Much to be learned, gained.
How far have you come?
Mere middling, I'm afraid.

I am from the death that birthed mourning,
leaving my mind in black of night.
In constant belief.
Had the right.
He returned, cursed monster,
to dance within my head.

Put me to bed.
Then fled.

I am from my sisters,
whose power and enlightenment took me from isolation.
His damning manipulation.
Lonely, but no longer alone.
Others share the story.
Shackled by legacy of pre-destiny.
Don't you stay
Be free!

I am from the drowning rains,
crafted by words taken from that wise book.
They cleanse, mend.
Mud from years of self scrutiny.
Leave stains.
Difficult to remove.
Here, a brush.
Scrub away the pains.

I am from the blade,
it slices as sharply as words crafted from my tongue.
Temporary Man.
He surges my imprisoned rage.
Why so angry?
For years his acts of tyranny.
Gifted me scorn.
Now injustice - no more!

I am from the crescent moon,

with its light of ambition I create new realities.
What is your fate, woman?
A decision not set.
In stone.
A journey, not destination.
Pictures not seen in cards.
MY manifestation.

I am from the fragile glass,
so transparent, I see clarity in the reincarnate.
Who are you?
I am Woman.
Closer to whom I was born to be.
You are not child, warrior?
Lover?
Why, I am all three.

I am from the phoenix,
a symbol for all those who tried to burn me.
Know I have risen.
No longer a pile of ashes.
Find your light yet?
Been running toward this thing.
But it lived within me, beside me.
This entire time.

Nicole Hawley is from Utica, NY. She's worked more than
19 years as a news reporter for a local daily newspaper. March
2019 she earned her MA in English/Creative Writing, summa
cum laude, from SNHU. Allpoetry.com/Nicole_Hawley

[Shane Ali]

Stir in the Night

A sun beam at midnight,
An unexpected warmth
Across my forsaken cheek.
Suddenly the universe
Laid bare at my feet,
And a silver lining
Sneaks into the space
Between my soul and dream.
Stirring me awake
As I float off to the stars.

It was your upside down kiss

This is my third published poem. Hope you enjoy my work.
My full book will be coming soon.
Across the Sea remains my favourite and was written for
Mithra. Hey you :) Allpoetry.com/Shane_Ali

[Catherine Jean Lindsey Towery Sales]
Education the Game Changer

Is a key that
Has open
many
Doors
for me.
What do I have
To show?
Five Beautiful educated
Children All of them know
Education is a Game changer
Be ready and willing
To stay on the go.

Education the Game Changer

Grateful to model
The dream
Mom don't need
anything.
My Attitude is Gratitude
For everything.
many lessons I learned
so Many Blessings .

Education, the Game Changer

Allowed me to raise children

In a safe environment
With Christian Values.
To teach other Children
To Get your education.
Education is the Game Changer
if you want knowledge
Go To college
if you dont want
to be otherwise
seek Wisdom.
Do not be wise
In your Own eyesight
Read your Bible
search for Wisdom
As if it's solid Gold
It will lead you to
The real Treasure
Learn to earn
and pay attention
before you seek
pleasure

EDUCATION THE GAME CHANGER

you ask me today
What has EDUCATION
Done for me?
It changed The game?
Taught me to think
before I speak.
To read and write

listen to learn
Test taking strategies
Conflict Resolutions
Problem solving Skills
To past down
from Generations
To Generations

Education The Game Changer

Does it teach
You how to be
A real wage earner
You may ask?
It's a real game
changer when
You are born
Into Poverty.
Remember Ignorance
Is no excuse to the law
stay in school
if you want to be cool
play by the rules
change the game
you do have a choice
Use your voice
And the pen which
is mightier than the
sword.
if you really want
To win,

Please look around
if you truly want to see
What education has
done for me.

Education, A,Game Changer

The list is too long
For me to go on
trust and believe

Education is a Game Changer

"I do believe if you can conceive, you will achieve."

The Game Changer is Education

Catherine Sales former Ed Counselor from Compton
CA.Catherine holds several Master's Degree in
Psychology,Education,Human Behavior,& Education Adm
Cred. Former President PA4C M.H .Advocacy 501C.
Allpoetry.com/Cathy_salesmft

[Stephen Hollins]

Lion Cub

1978 not a man or a child, but a Kiwi teenager
fishing for excitement and stimulation in Bali
not the five-star resorts with bars and spas

cocktails and peninsula perched swimming pools
surfer's villa, a bamboo hut, two dollars a night
first lunch melts in my mouth
'What is this?'
"Magic Mushrooms Mr."

flip-flops walking powdery sand, jeweled pebbles
giant coconut palms, bright green electric grass
cascading valleys, terraced rice paddy fields

smiling women in colorful sarongs and kabaya
blouses hurry along the street, bricks perched
high on their heads, smiling faces beaming joy

dusk falls, the beaches' turquoise coral waters turn
a dark shimmering silver, yellow moon peddles sky
a female with light cat feet pounces from darkness

have I walked into a mousetrap?
'Hey boy, you get a young woman tonight?'
she has several teeth missing and a wrinkled tanned face

I stutter and mumble as she darts her thin hand

under my testicles squeezing and lifting them
heartbeat races my organ her musical fingerboard

"you like?' she says, unlocking her firing grip
speechless with dropped jaw I nod yes, yes
ignited fibers in the fleshy groan singing a higher octave

'I get you a pretty girl, not me, you get
money, you bring back here; you go now, ok!'
my racing feet kick up sand
igniting thoughts of a bikini prostitute

eyes, breasts, silk, legs, kissing, melting into her
hand's, sweet lips of honey and ginger, fireworks
sex slave, Catholic guilt, jail, prison, torture

the excitement too much
for this man-child
head hits pillow

I am loving writing poetry I live on Waiheke Island New
Zealand. I specialize in Improv for Theatre, Acting,
Storytelling, Dance, Clown, Mime, Teaching, Building.
Allpoetry.com/Stephen_Hollins

[Sean Cooke]

Being a Flower

Imagine being a flower but you did not know, you were vibrant, and gave off a redolent smell that punctured the air with the winds turbulent flow.

Imagine if all you could feel was a child's gaze, the thud of a cats paw, and the glorious warmth of the suns rays.

Imagine the crystal like rain drops soaking you to the root, and avoiding the man made items that can transmute your form. Leaving you withered and wasted washed up by a storm.

Imagine if as seasons passed by like the hours on clocks, you adapted to nature's hardships and the pecking of birds that gathered in flocks.

Imagine as you gained confidence you blossomed and came into full vigour, you gave nature a mocking snigger.

Imagine if you felt so good you thought I can expand! Only for it to all end by you being picked by a delicate little child's hand.

I am a 29 year old man from northern England, It was the members of HART who got me into writing poetry. So I owe a lot to them. Allpoetry.com/Arsenalfan28

[Veronica Seals]

Rarity

I can feel the pain that flashes in my eyes
When I am told those three little words I used to despise
After years of being told such a lie
And being hurt so much that I just want to cry
All I can really think in my head is why?
In the end those three little words turn to four.
I love you, but...
...No...
Not that phrase again... Now I just try to ignore

Then here you come, almost breaking down my door
You had my mentality so twisted I had to sit on the floor and
think,
Do I want this anymore?
I'm glad, no thankful, that I made the choice I did
I almost ran and hid.

The man that I love is what I want, need and more.
The one i want to be my horizon on the shore.
The one who wants me to be me and nothing more.

I choose to feel life, not deny my humanity but embrace it.
Inhale the future, and exhale the past. Thank you to the man
who helped me see the possibilities for happiness in my life.
Allpoetry.com/Rsteel03

[Jackie C. Houk]

Everyone Wore Black

This truly was not a day for a funeral
The rain was beating down.
Everyone got soaked to the bone
As they put the casket in the ground.

They were all dressed in their finest black
As they came to say their last goodbye.
Over and over I heard
How he was such a good guy.

That's when I noticed her
Standing back among the trees.
Her black clothes clung tightly to her
Making her shiver in the breeze.

Why did she not come forward
To be with the others that were there?
I saw that she was gently crying
Letting me know that she truly cared.

Everyone was starting to leave
Now that the funeral was thru.
I went over to speak to her
To see what I could do.

We found a place to talk
That was out of the rain.

I put my black coat around her
And asked her for her name.

We talked for a while
Before she revealed that to me.
She was a daughter no one knew about
And the family likeness I could see.

Her mother worked as their maid
For oh so many years.
As she told the story about her Mom,
She had to stop and wipe away the tears.

The father of the house and her Mom
Had a short love affair.
Her Mom found out she was pregnant
And it gave her such a scare.

She quit her job and moved away
Not wanting to break up their home.
She never told him about me
She raised me on her own.

On her Mother's death bed
The truth was finally revealed.
She found out about her father
Her Mom's lips were no longer sealed.

She had met her father many times
Before today when the Lord called him home.
Now she had no one to turn to

She was left again all alone.

Let me talk to the family
And see what I can do.
I'm sure of what the outcome will be
They will open their arms to you.

They all fell in love with her right away
And she moved into their home.
Now she has a new family
And she will never again be alone.

Jackie Houk lives in Murfreesboro, Tennessee and is married to George. They have 2 sons. Jackie's first book, Rhymes With A Reason was published in 2017. She is currently working on her 2nd book. Allpoetry.com/Jackie_Houk

[Christopher Wry]

Eyes

They say they see all

but the mind will filter what

they and we will see

Just a 72 year old guy trying to keep my mind working.
Hopefully you will like my try. I live in New Hampshire.
Allpoetry.com/Christopher_Wry

[Dottie Crumbacker]

My Dad's Memory

Staring at the monitor,
as your life starts to fade away,
Has been the hardest moment
of my life up till this day.

Cool tears start to run,
like a marathon down my face.
My heart is beating louder,
as my pulse begins to race.

The room feels like it's getting warmer,
as I look and listen all around me.
It's as if I've suddenly forgotten,
how I'm supposed to breathe.

Then finally it has happened,
the line is completely flat.
I wish that there was something I could do;
To somehow bring you back.

I'd tell you one last time,
how much you mean to me.
And I hope I've made you proud,
in the time you got to see.

You will always be my hero,
and that will never change.

I will always be your baby,
no matter how old I age.

I wish that I could give you
just one more hug and kiss,
And tell you that I love you;
your spirit I will miss.

Until we meet again;
your memory lives on with me.
I will continue to make you proud
of the person I will be.

———————————

I am from Cecil County, MD. I've been writing poetry since elementary school. I enjoy writing poetry because it gives me a healthy creative outlet for my emotions and the events that occur in life. Allpoetry.com/Polkadot86

[Linda Burns]

My Morphine Owl

The surgery was over and I began to see
how the body might be better
but the pain was agony.
So I pushed my little "Nurse" thing
and one came strolling in.
I told her this is the worst pain I have ever been in.

She said "That is to be expected.
Are you allergic to morphine?"
I said "I don't know but if it will help,
I will try anything."

She took a device with a button and put in it my hand
saying push this when you need to. I need you to understand
push it no more than once a hour though it won't let you
overdose.
Don't let go now. Keep it close.

So I did and the pain completely went away
and as an added bonus I can truthfully say
I solved every problem that the human race had ever had.
I was happy and productive like a frog on a lily pad.

I wrote five books that had such logic and flow
from memories or hallucinations, I don't really know.
Problems were no longer problems because I knew
everything that should be said; everything that we should do.

266

It all just came together as I lay there in that bed.
I was amazed and grateful as ideas filled my head.
There came a time when they took my Morphine Owl away.
You have no idea how it hurts me when I have to say

that the books did not stay with me and the answers faded
as did, alas, the questions when not by morphine aided.
This sad story is a true one and I can't help but frown
for wishing I had been able to write all my visions down.

I was born two days after Christmas in 1946. I am from
Alabama by way of Texas. I am plain and simple and it's too
late to change now. Allpoetry.com/lindaburns

[Stephen Hollins]

Tulips glory

A single gold patterned napkin waltzes
like a limp crab across my table
I pour a babich merlot cabernet
its red figure deliriously dancing
into a large empty wine glass

René Aubry's – Plaisir's armor
super-sensitized my taste buds
as moon's face wordlessly quotes
some masterpiece invisible to me

upon opening the napkins
picture of a blue-gray Moscow
I scribe a note to the nervous
wide-eyed rats sitting at the Cuba shaped table

so far the clapping of crickets
and the nodding Canadian schoolboy
are the only witnesses present

clicking fingers like castanets I summon the bartender
a robust Vietnamese philosopher with a broad forehead
to deliver the napkin to the wide-eyed rats

his great enthusiasm to get involved and make the most
of this situation performing leaps, lounges, and pirouettes
from pillar to pillar as he swallows

half a dozen oysters, leaving quite an impression

he hands the note to Baby Tooth
the gang's leader and spells it out to them
in a series of deadly elevator kicks
they are "not welcome at mock zoo bar."

then the crickets go crazy as the Canadian
schoolboy keeps nodding his head
spilling my last sip of babich merlot cabernet
looking through the bottom of my glass
thirteen wavy sewer rats winding up fast
their little black mafioso figures gyrating in fury

outcomes their weapons and from under
my dark cloak tangos my trusty silver tulip

the bartender takes to cover
crickets make to the ceiling
while the Canadian schoolboy
keeps nodding

guns blaze in every direction
opium smoke fills the bar
bullets punch through the air
branding pulp fiction calligraphy
signatures on the walls

when the fog settles
and the last rat drops
I slowly turn to see the hole filled wall

to my astonishment, it reads the exact description
that I scribed on the note

"When death opens its door
you'll put on your carpet slippers
and stride on out of here -you dirty Rats."

I am loving writing poetry I live on Waiheke Island New
Zealand. I specialise in Improv for Theatre, Acting, Story
telling, Dance, Clown, Mime, Teaching, Building.
Allpoetry.com/Stephen_Hollins

[Vanja Petrushevska]

Vortex

Be somebody else
Be even better, that no one will guess
Whatever you imagine can come true
How far can you improve?

Wake up,
Stand up, breathe a new air
Find a better way
Make a good deed every day

Make better choices
Listen to all your positive voices
Be an example for your son
So he will make it when you are not around

Make everybody proud
You know that is not too hard...
I know...yeah...yeah ...you don't have time
But I can't understand what else is on your mind

Be happy, make someone happy
Oh my God, I'm so wealthy ...in a way how much I love my
life

Vanja Petrushevska LL.M in Intellectual Property Law, from Macedonia. Love to swim in the world of poetry, it's a food for my soul. Allpoetry.com/Time_in_the_Wind

[Wendy Stefanie Espinosa]

Queen of Hearts

She's not the brains but she is QUEEN
Has a terrible habit she can't kick
She's particular my heart I mean
To the worst kind she'd stick
She's got eyes of her own I can't control
& stops dead in her tracks for the rotten.
Her and brains should work as a whole
QUEEN tries but the rules get forgotten.

QUEEN drags us on this impossible task
A scavenger hunt a game she must pass
She accepts the challenge of wearing a mask
Mind Body and Soul searching the vulgar and crass.
Suddenly she sees, blindfold's on the ground
Closing her eyes scared to take a glance
Keeping them shut and feeling around
Frantically looking she can't lose her chance.
Determined to find the worthy and deserving.
The 4 leaf clover the needle in the hay.
While my brain's focused on conserving
It's been so long QUEEN'S gone astray.

I don't know what she's thinking.
Leaving us without a QUEEN.
While I just keep drinking.
& brain's pain wipes the scene.
She always gets lost on these missions.

Looking for something she can't prove is there.
I'm so dizzy and sick from the repetition.
Can't continue to partake in these affairs.
What is she trying to achieve?
Does she hate us, wants us to suffer?
Is she looking for something to believe?
Are these games just a buffer?
Looking for the best in the worst
thinking we're one in the same?
Needing to see it in someone first?
More questions then answers came...

Angrily calling out for our QUEEN
To pick us and love us
We made a mess only she can clean
& have so much we need to discuss
Look into us, we can blindfold you
We're the most important mission to crack.
Maybe our own quest you can get through.
Work hard for this and please just come back!

Wendy Stefanie is from New Jersey Nationality background is from Uruguay. Wendy started writing when she was 9 year old and continued to write into her adulthood. Wendy loves music and writing poetry Allpoetry.com/Feathered.

[Catherine Jean Lindsey Towery Sales]
America Justice

America Justice has none for me
It never was meant to be
America Justice only some you see
How dare you compare!
Your life to me
telling me about fairness
and complaining to me
telling how justice is fair
Fair is a place you go for fun
its not where America Justice is done
Stop your whining pretending not to see
What life has done for those who look just like me
How dare you Dream of hopes to be
America Justice not equality
My eyes may be close there not sleep
to America's Injustice if you are Brown, Black, or Red like me
My son, My son a Mother Cries!
"Judge not fair, reading all those lies,"
Twenty Five to life the Mother Cries, "WHY?"
It's called America's Justice so dry
those Weeping Eyes.
She has no Justice for you or me
And no she's not fair with Equality
Go back shouts America, to your Community
America Justice is not for you or me
Her Gold of here and Promises made

has never been yours nor mine
Her boarders of justice never really defined
Her Cries of Abundance
Fruits, nuts and Grains
doesn't feed our hunger
nor ease our pain
Her Proud Declaration are just leaves in the wind
Her Southern Borders Exposure Black Death Befriends
I have Discovered
America Justice is just Dead
With Centuries of Abuse
and barely being fed
She keeps her bright future
by Raping Black Souls
Entrapping the Children
with legends & History Untold
America Justice
has none for me.

Catherine Sales former Ed Counselor from Compton
CA.Catherine holds several Master's Degree in
Psychology,Education,Human Behavior,& Education Adm
Cred. Former President PA4C M.H .Advocacy 501C.
Allpoetry.com/Cathy_salesmft

[Gene Simia]

I Feel The Sea

Something more than wave or tide,
draws me to the bluest deep.
As if to beckon, my soul abides,
kept secrets in it's depths it weeps.

Tempestuous rhythms, surging power,
enthrall me in the sands of time.
Briny wisps, walls that tower,
run to the shore of maritime.

The songs of gulls, fill the air,
portraits of sound fill my ears.
Cries of hunger, the voice of a prayer,
that only the sea might hear.

Leviathan surfaces gracing my eyes,
lungs filled with air to dive.
Returning to the deep, he sighs
in a language, they know he arrives.

Dolphins play as the water pleads,
they beckon me to know their essence.
They smile as if their minds can read,
my curious acquiescence.

The shore awaits a mighty pour,
the ebb and flow as time-keep.

Life awash upon the basin floor,
sustenance for the brine deep.

Symphonic pulsations of blue and green,
change hue with motion and force.
Ears have not heard, nor eyes have seen,
such power with no remorse.

I feel the sea as it becomes me,
my spirit is quenched and nourished.
I become one with its beauty,
as I'm nurtured and encouraged.

Gene Simia makes his home in Munroe Falls, Ohio, along
with his wife Yvonne Simia. He is also a pianist,
percussionist and singer/songwriter. Yvonne writes children's
books and teaches art. Allpoetry.com/William_Pencraft

[Carlos Vargas]

Spring

For the longest time, I thought I wanted to be alone and I liked it. I enjoyed isolation. I never wanted to be found until someone prompts you to come out of your hiding place. It's like you're seeing the sun for first time and feeling its warmth on your skin, beauty in life comes into fruition. The snows have melted and you see parts of yourself you've never seen. The sutures in your heart have come undone, spilling and flowing like rivers. You're feeling as if it were the first time. My heart blooms like Spring because Winter is over.

I'm from Los Angeles, California. I'm a screenwriter, filmmaker, and a dreamer. Poetry always came as second nature to me, but I never fully explored it because I never had a muse. Until I met her. Allpoetry.com/Cheerupcharlie

[Connie S. Bradley]

God As My Partner

With God as my partner
I let go and let God
Lead me and guide me
To where I need to be
And to whom I need to see
And God speaks through me
My thoughts, My words,
My Behaviors, and Actions
Are of my highest Self
For the benefit of
All mankind

I begin each morning with gratitude and meditation with God.
For years I have made note of the quite unspoken messages
that come to me and now I share my favorite verses in
universal love with you. Allpoetry.com/CSBradley

[Lisa Gordon]

Ego

My words are my ego.
An ego so bound.
Bound to my insecurities.
Insecurities of which were not there.
Insecurities which hid my beauty. Beauty over looked.
Beauty degraded.
Beauty taken.
Taken by the egos of mongrels.
Hounds who clawed.
Hounds who scarred.
Scared said delicate ego.

My words are my ego.
An ego that searched.
Search for validation.
Validation which brought peace.
Peace of mind.
Peace within.
Peace engulfing hatred.
Hatred birthed from judgement. Judgment placed by hyenas.
Savages so vile.

My words are my ego
An ego that I fear will be shattered
Shattered by the venom of snakes.
Snakes that I once fed and nurtured.
Nurtured with love and gentleness. Gentleness that I yearned

for.
That I craved.
That I cut for.
Cut deeper than the skin.
Deeper than the tissue.
Deeper than the soul.
A soul so tortured,
The strongest love could not heal it
My words are my ego.
My words are my ego.
My words are my ego.

I'm a young writer, but my words reflect everything but that.
I've always been told that the best art comes from a place of
pain. For me that is true, my life is filled with pain. But I heal
by poetry Allpoetry.com/Gordol11

[Blair Bryant]
Wise Owl Volume II

Your blonde hair to silver with a blink
underneath that old owl
where darkness cast shadows on oak.

I could see my grandchildren in your eyes.

You make me complete with every blink
with one small glimpse
I saw two little souls!

An old owl danced to the view,
Hoot! Hoot!

For the Lord sent him
the bearer of our good news.

Allowing me to see vision's
of my children's children
in your morning blue eyes.

I saved the old owl
from drowning in the muddy river.

How he fell in, I don't know how?
I only could hear
Hoot! Hoot!

Animals see the spirit realm.
We humans lost the ability to see.

Lost the eyes of truth
when Adam and Eve were cast
from the Garden.

The old owl wanted to repay me
and asked the Lord to give him
vision's on his wings.

To carry in his voice
With each, Hoot! Hoot!

I could see the spectacular happening!

All at once
in her eyes
as the sun finally faded.

I pulled her in, kissing my sweet love
her cherry sweet kiss.

I feel her every heartbeat
thanking the Lord for the truth!
I just smiled at the wise old owl
He flew off, to where?
Maybe to a far away mysterious view?

I only could hear,
Hoot! Hoot!

I'm from Powhatan Virginia. I enjoy writing, it's relaxing. Love riding horses and some blueberry pancakes....
Allpoetry.com/Blair_Bryant

[Roshan John]

She was talking

Sometimes it's better
To watch you talk
Move those lips
In hundred ways
Roll those eyes
Express your inner self
I would rather be mute
Listen to all that you offer
Because I'm no judge
Of your chatter
I love to see you active
Filling the air with energy
This world needs sound
From beautiful souls.

_____

Roshan John is from Kochi , the Queen of the Arabian Sea .
He likes fishing and is a physician by profession . Poetry is
his release and long time passion.
Allpoetry.com/Roshan_John

[Audrey Seybold]

Illuminate

the world is cold
but your heart is warn
so rise up from the ashes
and march through the madness

darkness doesn't last forever
don't waste the days waiting for a savior

you can illuminate the gray
and shine brighter than the sun
carry on until the battle is won
because your life isn't one to waste

carry on until the battle is won
you can illuminate the gray
and shine brighter than the sun

darkness doesn't last forever
look in the mirror, there's your savior

we never know what tomorrow brings
sometimes a new challenge
sometimes a new blessing
and away goes the madness

darkness doesn't last forever
so carry on, soldier

Audrey Seybold is a model, poet, and artist from New York, New York. She loves creative writing, poetry and comedy. Allpoetry.com/AudreySeybold

[Dominic Houlihan]

Broken hearts

When you said your last goodbyes.
A part of me died inside.
The pain I felt my eye's couldn't hide.
With the thoughts without you by my side.

You left without a glance.
Was something I will never understand.
How once you stood in front of me
And told me I was your other half.

As weeks went on I watched it move
Behind your eye's.
The taste of betrayal your face could
No longer hide.

Even knowing what you done
Still makes it so much harder
In moving on.
And I know it won't be easy to
Walk away.
But I have to let you go.
It will hurt for a while
But I know ill be fine.
Because i know I have let go.

Because my heart deserves to

Belong too someone new.
And in someone else's hands.

Dominic Houlihan is from Co Kerry Ireland. Poetry is one of
the best ways to feel and get so much emotions across through
your pen Allpoetry.com/Dominichoulihan

[Lisa F. Raines]
Our Retreat

You kissed me,
So soft and so sweet.
I miss you,
Still feeling your heat.

I listen,
For the fall of your feet.
Our tryst is
A beautiful retreat.

Near the abyss,
As we so entreat,
God's love and his bliss,
Please make us complete.

AlisRamie is from North Carolina, USA.
Interests include: philosophy, history, international relations,
poetry, art, design, jazz, funk, and some good old soul.
Allpoetry.com/AlisRamie

[Lisa F. Raines]

Denial

I'm broken ---- I'm not broken
I'm broken ---- I am not broken

I'm broken ---- It's a thought disorder.
I'm broken ---- What's a thought disorder?

I'm broken ---- Is there any help?
I'm broken ---- I'm not broken!

I'm broken ---- Who can help me?
I'm broken ---- I'm broken?

I'm broken ---- Can you help me?
I'm broken ---- What broke?

I'm broken ---- Who am I?
I'm broken ---- Who broke me?

I'm broken ---- Why?
I'm broken ---- I'm not broken.

AlisRamie is from North Carolina, USA.
Interests include: philosophy, history, international relations,
poetry, art, design, jazz, funk, and some good old soul.
Allpoetry.com/AlisRamie

[Sandra Joann Ray]

Broken Heart

I brought my broken heart to God for only
he could mend
The thought of losing my Dad
was too difficult for this child to comprehend!

I was so young when you died
I didn't know what to do
I struggled each day to understand
and find my way through

I use to sit and pretend
some mistake had been made
and somehow you would walk
through that door and
I would no longer be afraid

I finally had to admit to myself
that you were truly gone
all this pretending didn't do a thing for me
I just had to move on

I learned to look at death
and just move on my way
take a deep breath and hope to God
He would spare everyone else along the way

I came to know a God

who was a Father to the fatherless
one who truly cared
A God who never left you
one who was always there

A God I came to love
with all of my heart
A God who stands in the gap
when you have a broken heart

I know one day I will see you
and tell you things I never got to say
But until then Dad, know that
I love you more and more each day

Sandra Joann Ray is from Fremont, Ohio. Poetry helps me express myself and cope with the storms of my life. I use my poetry to testify of the unconditional love, amazing grace and goodness of God! Allpoetry.com/Sandrasmilesagain1

[Jemma M]
Shrink

Power and hope lost in this room of Shrink,
Crazy and lazy, no ability to think.
Agitation. Sedation.
Depression. Repression.
Ignore the mood.
Deprived of food.

Two pm, Tuesday in this room of Shrink,
Smiling so pretty and dressed in pink.
Cries. Lies.
Acts. Retracts.
Flatter the Shaper.
Accept the paper.

Control and secrets, hidden in this room of Shrink,
They think she looks good; it's not what they think.
Cigarettes. Lost bets.
Gut rots. Coffee pots.
Vanish she hopes.
Shrink is how she copes.

Jemma M is from Vancouver, BC. Poetry has been the best therapy in my experience. I'm always open to the journey of learning, guidance, and self improvement.
Allpoetry.com/Jemma_M

[Joshua Gabriel Horsey]
Golden Age

I see them in full: These beings of discourse. They like to
show who does worse. When I use my eyes to find honesty,
they are always met with greater pleasure and debauchery.
Though, they claim to bare true heart; I see a flesh collected in
scars. Words hide of masked want, using scents to taunt. I
myself witness the birth; of beings who carry morals as strong
as dirt. And, when light comes to save; those trapped in their
indulgence rather shade.

A modern Libertine, and rogue philosopher. Joshua hails
from Philadelphia, Pa. " The highest ethic of a writer should
be to write what is true, and not what is good".
Allpoetry.com/J_G_Horsey

[Manvi Goel]

A quirk in dunkirk

Two lone roads coalescing into one,
beating the bushes for a pal
to walk, run and giggle with fun.
The pal standing inert on the crossway,
fighting for a breath in an airy grave enswathed with dismay,
rubbing his eyeballs with the panoramic view,
gauging the winks of ethereal clues,
held his sight for a while
on a fact,
that was intact,
the twain equivalently laid towards an end,
where lied another untold story to be penned.
Which path to tread the heels on,
which to walk out on,
this pendulum of dilemma was oscillating round the clock,
yodeling tick tock tick tock,
coding decoding multifaceted blocks into blocks.
The path worn by the ages of divergent strides,
that turned greyish black from white and sapphire across the
miles,
was looking upon him with a smirk,
winking him to chase with a jerk.
In such a quandary,
a wobbling mind and a throbbing heart,
was left high and dry,
yearning for a quirk in dunkirk.
Amidst the whirl of a thwarting tussle,

when the immortal of the mortal,

clapped its eyes on the scintillating gem of immortal,

the misty briny deep,

took a long breathe,

with the symphony,

of an epiphany,

crossroads are the chords of death and life,

one way leads to another way of strife,

no way is wrong or right,

each has its own journey of a unique thrive,

the roads onto roads and the crossroads,

will some day lead to a dead end,

with kaleidoscopic contours delineating infinite ocean's
strand,

while the realms of mortality,

converge with the realms of immortality,

the two unalike roads,

paving the way to divers of unalike roads,

meet at their confluence,

loosing their individuality in congruence,

and unveiling an essence,

it's the traveler and his aesthetic sense,

that honours the roads with the facet of an apple and oranges
unalikeness.

With this acoustic awareness,

the spirited elan vital

took the path less trodden,

a road not many had chosen,

a path where the swans were flying on the ether,

engraving their pearly sapient footprints that never wither,

escorting him from miles to miles,

with a drizzle of prismatic smiles.
The pal murmured to the recesses of his heart,
Oh!! I don't want to apologize,
for giving my ears to a seraphic voice,
and not trailing around with a congested advice,
as it is a journey of my strive,
a journey of my variegated detours,
an odyssey of revamping my contours,
a drive of transcendental rides,
an expedition towards blooming with a charisma that is
sublime.

I am from India. I am a nature lover. I love being artistic and
exploring the unexplored things in this world. I believe in
living alive every moment of life,. Love your life, life will
love you back Allpoetry.com/Manvi_Goel

[Lisa F. Raines]

Weapons and War

Weapons of war,
mountains of gore,
"a glorious tour"?

The world before,
cannons galore,
cannot restore,

the truth in store.
The need for more,
for rich and poor,

must not ignore,
makes us endure,
what they abhor.

What is our core?
Where is the floor?
How many more?

They're at the door!
Alone no more,
since 1984...

AlisRamie is from North Carolina, USA.
Interests include: philosophy, history, international relations,
poetry, art, design, jazz, funk, and some good old soul.
Allpoetry.com/AlisRamie

[Jemma M]

Journey back to home

You were born of dreams
You were created from true love
Forever and always you will be our children
Adoration and connection from the first meeting of our eyes
Admiration and acceptance continuing throughout our lives

We are travelling a journey
That is many times difficult to navigate
Sometimes feeling lost, without a compass to guide
Trying to reconcile time passed
Recreating the story of the past

Blue skies, sunshine, thunder and lightening
Atmospheric tension and unpredictable connection
Also gentle waters, and a secure shelter to dwell
You are our children, now adults
We were adults, but children as well

All of us are human
Vulnerable yet strong
Fallible yet growing
Brave yet sometimes scared
Desiring love, value, protection
appreciation and affection

The best was, and is, always wanted for you
We may show it differently, separately, not the same

300

We've made mistakes in both behaviour and action
It's with heartfelt remorse that we have caused you pain
It's in loving agreement, you are the greatest gifts life ever
gave

Sometimes the path for two needs to divide
In order to reach the same destination
Even if that means life in a different location
The journey of love is always true
Our hearts will always be a home for you

Jemma M is from Vancouver, BC. Poetry has been the best
therapy in my experience. I'm always open to the journey of
learning, guidance, and self improvement.
Allpoetry.com/Jemma_M

[D'atrice Stephens]
Love in its most purest form

You know that feeling of a sensational bliss?
That feeling of knowing
that this particular being is your person,
your muse, your reason for smiling,
being happy and glowing?

Can I ask that you feel me up with your rawest emotions?
I want to be the reason your smile won't fade
I want to be the light that'll always light your way.
The sun to your moon the rainbow after the rain..

Let's keep each other lifted and guided,
honoring our pasts that have led us to this very moment
where we can finally be free from the world of chaos
vibing on levels to create our own galaxy.

It's no mistake that your energy ignites with mine
we have a love that's meant to last for a lifetime.
I remember the visions,
the dreams I used to have.
Not knowing that it was you whose attention I had to grab.

Let's be love baby,
let's be peace together
let's ride this wave of eternal bliss together.

I thank you already even though I don't really know you

but I always knew that it was a you that I had to get to.

So hold on.
Let's not give up just yet.
Let's keep the faith alive that we'll be dwelling
in each other's love
waking up and watching the sun rise.

Gazing out at the stars at night.
Basking in what's pure what's meant to be
just for us.

I'm from Albany, GA, but now live in Florida. I'm a mother
of a beautiful little girl. I love writing and creating poetry
because I'm always looking for ways to help people heal.
Peace, Light, Love. Allpoetry.com/Shantedee1990

[Curtis Lee Turner Jr.]

Love Hurts

Sad how it happen emotions, and feelings caught me off guard
A little more insight, I would have played another card
when I look back, I noticed I was in too deep emotions
and feelings was depriving me of my sleep.

I couldn't rest it seems like, I was always preparing for a test
that, I could never pass, a matter of fact no one could pass
my final grade F. When I noticed two months later
your love had left.

Fighting not to be that player, and hurt you, but unsolved
feelings left me exposed with a clue.
reduced down to casual friends, maybe this is how we were
scheduled to end.

Seal up all our good memories for your stories down the road
and know, love can't die, even when we get old.

Thewriterc lives in Columbus, Ohio writing since the age of
12 years old. Songs, commercials jingles, and working on my
screenplay for films. I believe poetry is born in the heart and
mind.

Allpoetry.com/Thewriterc

[Sandra Joann Ray]

A Strong Mom who gave All

Your life wasn't as easy
as you'd hoped it may be
Losing the love of your life
And being left with 3

Being a single parent
Was never part of the plan
Sometimes things in life happen
That we never understand

The struggles that you faced and the storms
That you made it through
Were a testament of what a strong Mom can do

How can we ever repay you
For giving us all you had
Taking your place as Mom
And also as Dad

Sandra Joann Ray is from Fremont, Ohio. Poetry helps me express myself and cope with the storms of my life. I use my poetry to testify of the unconditional love, amazing grace and goodness of God! Allpoetry.com/Sandrasmilesagain1

[Jemma M]

Broke

Broken trust, splintering home
Broken words on a telephone.
Security a foundation and truth a proclamation
Sweeping silently away in a sea of damnation.

We made a deal, my dear old friend
A promise meant to be kept until the end.
Each had a role we were meant to take
Now those roles are about to break.

Swearing on my life and the life of your child,
Seem to mean nothing and make my thoughts run wild.
Broken security and broke in the bank,
Letters and calls, pop another tranq.

Broken truths lie larger than love
Seemingly salvageable as a dead dove.
Another year of debt in love and money,
Broken apart again, perhaps it's funny.

Smile and laugh with a glass of wine,
It's all a façade, as we'll see next time.
Too broken to honor one another's presence,
Too broke to buy anniversary presents.

Reality sets in yet once again,
Broken apart, with no one to blame.

Jemma M is from Vancouver, BC. Poetry has been the best therapy in my experience. I'm always open to the journey of learning, guidance, and self improvement.
Allpoetry.com/Jemma_M

Made in the USA
Lexington, KY
05 July 2019